EYE OF THE WHIRLWIND

THE STORY OF JOHN SCOPES

BY D.C. IPSEN

DRAWINGS BY RICHARD CUFFARI

Addisonian Press Titles
by D. C. Ipsen
THE ELUSIVE ZEBRA
RATTLESNAKES AND SCIENTISTS
THE RIDDLE OF THE STEGOSAURUS
WHAT DOES A BEE SEE?

 An Addisonian Press Book

Addison-Wesley Publishing Company, Inc.
Reading, Massachusetts 01867
Printed in the United States of America
First Printing

HA/HA

Library of Congress Cataloging in Publication Data
Ipsen, D C
    Eye of the whirlwind   the story of John Scopes
    SUMMARY: Recounts the life of John Thomas Scopes and his trial of
1925 which tested the right of a teacher to teach evolution.
    "An Addisonian Press book."
    1. Scopes, John Thomas. 2. Evolution—Juvenile literature. [1. Scopes,
John Thomas. 2. Evolution. 3. Teachers] I. Cuffari, Richard, 1925–
illus.
II. Title.
KF224.S317   345'.73'0288 [B] [92]   72-4777
ISBN 0-201-03172-8

CONTENTS

iii

Note About Sources

Of the many accounts used as reference for this book, John Scopes's memoirs (notably *Center of the Storm* by Scopes and Presley) were considered a primary source, especially for the events of his life before and after the summer of 1925.

But for that eventful summer, day-by-day accounts were largely relied upon. A court stenographer recorded the many words of the Scopes trial as they were spoken. And daily stories in such newspapers as the New York *Times,* the New Orleans *Times-Picayune,* and the San Francisco *Chronicle* provided immediate impressions of events in and out of the courtroom, capturing some of the color and excitement of the scene.

PREFACE

John Scopes always insisted that he was an ordinary man caught up in extraordinary events. He was born into the family of a railroad mechanic. He died an oil-company geologist. But in between he became the central figure—"the center of the storm," he called himself in his memoirs—in one of the world's most famous courtroom dramas, the Tennessee Evolution Trial.

In any account of Scopes's life, the trial that gave him his fame naturally occupies a prominent position. And fortunately that 1925 event was reported in great detail. Over a hundred reporters squeezed into the Dayton, Tennessee, courtroom that was the scene of the "Monkey Trial." And thousands of words were telegraphed each day to newspapers throughout the country—and beyond. But the copious reports of the trial have sometimes made the story of those days less certain rather than more so. The numerous observers frequently came away with different memories of just what had happened during those hot summer days in Dayton.

From the many accounts, I have tried to sort out the truth. But sometimes the truth has had to be guessed. And in that guessing I may sometimes have guessed wrong. I may have placed a gesture or a grimace or even a conversation in the wrong place or the wrong time. I may even have seen truth in some pleasant fiction. But the story of past events must always be partly uncertain. Even the story of man's creation, as the Scopes trial demonstrated, can be disputed.

D.C.I.

CHAPTER ONE
THE SUBSTITUTE

Central High School in Dayton, Tennessee, had a good football team in 1924. It wasn't the best high-school team in Tennessee, or even the second best. But it was good enough to beat the second-best team. At least that was the coach's opinion as their game against that team entered its final minutes.

Dayton, Tennessee, was a pleasant town of around 1800 inhabitants lying in the Tennessee River Valley about forty miles upstream from Chattanooga. It was not actually on the river but back toward the mountains to the west. When the town began, iron ore was being taken from the mountains. But the mines were no longer being worked to speak of. Now Dayton was the center of a farming region. Strawberries were a big crop. Also big was corn, which was probably used mostly for making whiskey. But in 1924 making whiskey was against the law, and nobody kept track of just where the corn crop went.

Dayton was the county seat of Rhea County, and Central High was the county's one high school. Many of the students came from the surrounding farms to go to school in Dayton. And they brought their farming muscles to the football team.

In football, though, Central High's biggest asset was a boy named Punk Cunningham. Punk was a dangerous runner and also a deadly drop-kicker. In 1924 drop-kicking was an important part of football. It was a common way to kick a field goal. The kicker dropped the ball to the ground in front of him and then kicked it just as it bounced up.

In their game against their big rival, Central High had managed to close the first half in a tie. Now in the second half they had moved the ball deep into enemy territory. The coach decided it was time to send in Punk. He gave Punk instructions for the quarterback: two plays into the line to draw in the defense, then a wide end run with Punk carrying the ball. If that didn't work, Punk could kick a field goal on fourth down.

The plays into the line served their purpose. And Punk's wide end run on third down was brilliant. But there was someone in the way who managed to pull him to the turf short of the goal. Their field position was now so good, though, that a field goal from the sure toe of Punk Cunningham was almost automatic.

On fourth down the center snapped the ball to Punk. Almost casually he went through the motions of kicking the field goal. But to the shock of his teammates and the coach, the ball glanced off the side of his toe and into the outstretched hands of an opponent. Central High had lost their great opportunity—and the ball. They went on to lose the game.

It was weeks later that the coach, John Scopes, learned how Punk had come to do the impossible—to miss that easy field goal. As he picked himself up from the third-down run he had made, Punk spied a dime in the grass. Of course he had to pick it up. But he had no pocket to put it in, and so he had the dime gripped in his hand as he attempted the field goal on the next play. His grip on the football was naturally somewhat awkward with the dime interfering. He dropped the ball badly and could not kick it well. Lamented Scopes, "If love of money is the root of all evil, we had, that afternoon, one of the costliest dime's worth of proof in the history of football."

John Scopes, the athletic coach of Central High School, was a newcomer to Dayton, Tennessee, though not to the South. He was born in the neighboring state of Kentucky at the point where the meandering Tennessee River eventually reaches the Ohio. In Paducah, Kentucky, on August 3, 1900, Mary Scopes gave birth to a son. It was her fifth child but her first boy. The boy was given the name of John Thomas Scopes, with his middle name coming from his father.

Born as the nineteenth century was ending, John Scopes was destined to play a part in a drama that had its beginning earlier in that century. In 1859, Charles Darwin, an inconspicuous English scientist, had made the common man aware of an exciting—and, to some, disturbing—idea called evolution. In 1925, John Scopes, an inconspicuous American schoolteacher, would give the common man a new awareness of this exciting and disturbing idea.

John Scopes often said it all wouldn't have happened but for his father. By the common definition, Thomas Scopes was a Cockney. He was born within the sound of Bow bells—the bells of the church of St. Mary-le-Bow in London. But Thomas Scopes decided to see America before he settled down. He never got back to London except for a visit. In America he became a machinist for the railroads.

Thomas Scopes was something of a rebel. He became much involved with fighting for the rights of the worker. And surely some of his crusading spirit rubbed off on his son.

The city of Paducah, where John was born, came to mean home to the Scopeses, even though they were forced to live elsewhere during John's teenage years. When Thomas Scopes retired in 1922, it was to Paducah that he returned. But in between, the family, following the demands of a railway machinist's job, made several moves. In 1913 they moved to Danville, in east-central Illinois, then two years later to Salem, in southern Illinois.

There was a crazy coincidence in John Scopes's move to Salem that he couldn't recognize at the time. For that small Illinois town was the birthplace of William Jennings Bryan, the man who would one day make the name John Scopes known throughout the country if not the world.

Bryan had grown famous as a champion of the common man. Whatever the common man favored, the Great Commoner, as he came to be called, favored. Three unsuccessful campaigns for the United States presidency, though, convinced him that common men weren't common enough.

Bryan was born in Salem in 1860 but left his home town after his schooling, settling eventually in Lincoln, Nebraska. But he made it a point to return to Salem often to deliver a speech at one occasion or another. One occasion was John Scopes's graduation from high school in the spring of 1919.

Scopes always remembered that event as the time when the silver-tongued William Jennings Bryan made a remarkable slip of the tongue. Actually, it might have gone unnoticed if it hadn't been for the farewell sermon at the high school. One of the rituals of graduating from Salem High School was a special sermon for the graduating seniors given by a local minister. During the sermon Scopes sat with three friends who had been constant companions during their senior year.

The sermon was surely full of good advice to the graduating seniors. But Scopes and his friends had trouble paying attention to its message. The minister, it happened, had false teeth that gave a whistling sound at each word that ended in an *s.*

As the *s*'s whistled by, the four friends couldn't help but exchange smiles—then snickers. And so by the time the minister quoted two lines of verse that both ended with *s,* the friends couldn't control themselves. "Come with me into the bogs/ And hear the croaking of the frogs," the minister intoned, and the four companions burst into uncontrolled laughter.

It was a week later that William Jennings Bryan addressed the graduating class, and the same four who had disrupted the sermon were together in the front row. Bryan's speech, of course, would not be expected to be punctuated by whistles. Far from it. "He was one of the most perfect speakers I have heard," said Scopes; "he was nearly always flawless in every way." And so it was wholly unexpected when he uttered a word that ended in a loud

*Not knowing what had caused the laughter, Bryan simply
stared hard at the culprits.*

and clear whistling sound. The four friends couldn't avoid
a fresh outbreak of laughter. Not knowing what had
caused the eruption, Bryan simply stared hard at the four.
The great orator's spell had been broken only for a moment, but Bryan would recall that strange incident years
later in Dayton.

After high school, Scopes took five years getting
through college, instead of the usual four. The delay was
mostly caused by bronchitis, which plagued him during
his early college years. He started at the University of
Illinois but after his first year switched to the University
of Kentucky in hopes of finding the climate gentler on his
tender windpipe. The new climate was no help, and Scopes
was forced to drop out of college for a while. But he
returned to Kentucky later to complete his studies.

When Scopes graduated in 1924, he had a strange collection of subjects in his background. He had taken
courses from professors he liked without caring much
where they led. In the end he found he had taken enough
courses in law to call that a major, even though they
weren't enough to give him a law degree and permit him
to become a lawyer. He had, though, taken enough
courses in education to qualify him to teach school. As it
turned out, a clash between law and education would be
the central event of his life.

If the job opening at Central High School in Dayton
had happened earlier in the year, Scopes would probably
not have been hired to fill it. The school's athletic coach
had resigned in the late summer, and there was little time

to find a replacement. Even then, Scopes didn't look like a good candidate. "Slight, blond, soft-spoken, boyish" were words a reporter would later use to describe him. He looked more the scholar than the athlete. Horn-rimmed glasses were usually in place before his thoughtful blue eyes. But he had a lanky frame and had played basketball during his senior year in high school in Salem. And more important, the coach was also expected to teach some algebra, physics, and chemistry, and Scopes's background was good in those areas.

Scopes fit easily into the life of Dayton. He was well liked by his students and generally got along well with the older members of the community. Some did feel that he set a bad example for his students by his smoking. And the more religious felt that a schoolteacher shouldn't be seen dancing with the girl students at the Saturday night dances. But he was still well thought of, and his position in Rhea County Central High School in Dayton looked secure.

There was little in Scopes's life in Dayton that foreshadowed his role in the great battle over evolution that was to come. Certainly the coaching and teaching that he was hired for had nothing to do with evolution. The athletics program naturally had no concern with the origins of life. Nor did the mathematics program. And even the science that had been assigned to Scopes would not be expected to call for any mention of biologist Charles Darwin or the theory that he had proposed. So if Scopes had merely carried out the job he was hired to do, he would surely have lived and died unknown to the world.

But in the spring of 1925, as his first year of teaching was running out, Scopes had a small job thrust upon him that changed his life. The principal of the school became ill during the last few weeks of school. A part of the principal's job was teaching biology. Scopes was asked to fill in. He had some background, and besides, all the class was doing was reviewing for the final exam. That little review job was to start Scopes on an adventure he would never forget.

CHAPTER TWO
THE DRUGSTORE
PLOT

His first year of teaching ended on May 1, and John Scopes had plans to go home to Paducah to visit his family for the summer of 1925. But for one small reason or another he stayed on in Dayton for a few days, filling his time with swimming and tennis.

It was during a game of tennis that he got a message to come to Robinson's Drugstore—"if it's convenient." Scopes guessed that Doc Robinson, who was also head of the school board, had some school matter to talk about. And so at the end of the game he walked downtown to the store, still steaming from his exertion. In early May it was already warm in Dayton.

When Scopes reached the drugstore, he found half a dozen men at one of the tables near the soda fountain. They appeared to be in the midst of a lively discussion as he joined them. Doc Robinson pulled up another wire-backed chair for him and sent the soda jerk after a cool drink. A couple of the town's lawyers were present, along with three more of the town's citizens who were familiar to Scopes.

One of these was George Rappleyea, a mining engineer who lived in Dayton. He was a nervous man with a shock of black hair that was starting to turn gray though he was still in his thirties. He had come from New York and had never quite been accepted by the citizens of Dayton.

"John," asked Doc Robinson, "would you be willing to stand for a test case?"

Rappleyea was the first to speak: "John, we've been arguing and I said that nobody could teach biology without teaching evolution."

"That's right," Scopes said. Then seeing questions in some of the faces about him, he grabbed a copy of Hunter's *Civic Biology* from a nearby shelf. Hunter was the text that had been used in high-school biology courses in Tennessee for many years. It was supplied to the Rhea County students through Robinson's Drugstore.

Scopes showed the men clustered about the drugstore table the part in the book dealing with evolution, including the diagram showing the descent of man from earlier non-human animals.

"You have been teaching them this book?" Rappleyea asked. Scopes admitted he had. After all, it was the text.

"Then you've been violating the law," chimed in Doc Robinson.

Scopes took the news as calmly as it was given. If he had thought about it during his days as a substitute biology teacher, he probably would have realized that he was breaking the law. But he hadn't thought about it.

It wasn't that he hadn't heard of the Butler Act, which was the name the antievolution law was known by. He just had never worried about it. Who had? The Butler Act had passed the Tennessee House of Representatives by a 71 to 5 vote and the Tennessee Senate by 24 to 6. Most of the legislators thought it was a hard act for them to vote against. It would be like voting against the Bible, which wasn't the thing for a politician to do in most parts of

Tennessee. But they didn't take the act too seriously. On March 21, six weeks before the end of school, the governor of the state had signed it into law, saying as he did so: "Probably the law will never be applied."

The Butler Act was short and simple—about as short and simple as a legal document can be, anyway. The first section of the act did take a long time to get to the point. "BE IT ENACTED BY THE GENERAL ASSEMBLY OF THE STATE OF TENNESSEE, That it shall be unlawful for any teacher in any of the Universities, Normals and all other public schools of the State which are supported in whole or in part by the public school funds of the State," it began. But the punch line was brief: "to teach any theory that denies the story of the Divine Creation of man as taught in the Bible, and to teach instead that man has descended from a lower order of animals."

The second section set the penalty for such a misdeed. "BE IT FURTHER ENACTED," it read, "That any teacher found guilty of the violation of this Act shall be guilty of a misdemeanor and upon conviction, shall be fined not less than One Hundred ($100.00) Dollars nor more than Five Hundred ($500.00) Dollars for each offense."

The last section called for hasty enforcement: "BE IT FURTHER ENACTED, That this Act take effect from and after its passage, the public welfare requiring it."

As Doc Robinson calmly suggested that his friend John Scopes was a law-breaker, he handed him a copy of the Chattanooga *News* and pointed to an item. The ACLU—

the American Civil Liberties Union—was offering to pay the expenses of anyone who would agree to test the constitutionality of the Butler Act.

As it is today, the ACLU was then in the business of seeing to it that the rights of any person are not ignored —especially rights protected by the Constitution. The Butler Act, the ACLU felt, denied the teacher and the students rights that are guaranteed to all citizens, and so it should be declared unconstitutional. The way to get that done was to get someone to break it—to make a test case. That would get the law into the courtroom where a decision about its constitutionality would be made.

"John," asked Robinson, "would you be willing to stand for a test case?"

Scopes didn't hesitate long: "If you can prove that I taught evolution, and that I can qualify as a defendant, then I'll be willing to stand trial."

Robinson quizzed him: "You filled in as a biology teacher, didn't you?"

"Yes," agreed Scopes, "when Mr. Ferguson was sick."

"Well, you taught biology then. Didn't you cover evolution?"

Scopes stopped to think. "We reviewed for final exams, as best as I can remember."

Robinson, undisturbed by his vague answer, walked to the phone and called the Chattanooga *News*. "This is F. E. Robinson in Dayton," he said when the connection was made. "I'm chairman of the school board here. We've just arrested a man for teaching evolution."

Scopes finished the coke he had been handed during the discussion and went back to the high school to resume his tennis match. But the die had been cast. The fates of Scopes and of Dayton were to take a turn that probably neither would have predicted—surely not John Scopes.

CHAPTER THREE
A TALE
OF TWO BOOKS

The collision between John Scopes and the law had been in the making for some time—thousands of years, in fact. There is no record of when people began to believe that the first man was created out of dust by God. But the story was written down by an unknown Hebrew living somewhere between the Dead Sea and the Mediterranean some eight hundred or so years before the birth of Christ. Now, almost three thousand years later, that event would send John Scopes into a hot Tennessee courtroom.

The words of that ancient writer were copied many times over the centuries and were combined with the words of many other religious writers. And they were translated into many languages. When the words finally reached the hills of Tennessee, they were in the language of the time of King James the First of England: "And the Lord God formed man of the dust of the ground, and breathed into his nostrils the breath of life; and man became a living soul."

To many Tennesseans, these words were easily recognized as chapter 2 verse 7 of the book of Genesis. They were a part of their unfailing guide to thought and action, the Holy Bible. And they were words, they felt, that should guide the thought and action of John Scopes as well.

The hills of Tennessee in 1925 were well populated with a variety of Christians that had come to be called "fundamentalists." They prided themselves in being simple people with simple wants, and they prided themselves in having a simple religion. All it required was that they believed the Bible—every word of it. In their view, the Bible was the word of God. Even though it may have been written down by human beings, those special beings who did the job were always inspired by God. And so it was just as if God were writing it.

Fundamentalism got an early start in America. It came over on the *Mayflower*. The Pilgrims didn't use that name to describe their religion, but it would have fit. And so fundamentalism surely was, as it was often called, "that old-time religion."

But the surge of fundamentalism that was to carry Scopes into court was a recent thing. It had begun after World War I and had been helped along by many who were confused and dismayed by the direction the world seemed to be heading. A return to old ways—especially to that old-time religion—looked like the best cure for the ills of the world.

Fundamentalism probably got its biggest boost from William Jennings Bryan, the man who had addressed John Scopes's high-school graduation class in Salem, Illinois. Bryan was a great speaker, of course, and when he started speaking in favor of fundamentalism, he found many who would listen.

Bryan had first shown the country what a speaker he was back in 1896. In that year he had gone to the Democratic presidential convention as a 36-year-old delegate from Lincoln, Nebraska. Bryan's main ambition was to talk the convention into adopting a platform that favored having silver made into coins as freely as gold was at that time. In a spellbinding oration that has come to be known as the Cross of Gold speech, Bryan urged: "You shall not press down upon the brow of labor this crown of thorns. You shall not crucify mankind upon a cross of gold!" The convention responded by making Bryan the Democratic candidate for president.

The Cross of Gold speech was only the beginning. Bryan traveled 18,000 miles through 27 states giving 600 speeches along the way trying to convince the voters of America that he should be the next man in the White House. But it didn't work. He lost the election to William McKinley, the Republican candidate.

Bryan, though, was never one to be dismayed by defeat. If that was God's will, he would accept it.

Bryan had to accept defeat twice more. He ran against McKinley in 1900 and again lost. Then in 1908 he was the unsuccessful Democratic candidate for the third time, that time against William Howard Taft.

Bryan didn't try for the presidency again. But he did remain a force in Democratic politics. He is given credit for getting Woodrow Wilson nominated in 1912. When Wilson went on to win the election, Bryan became Secretary of State in Wilson's cabinet. But for the Great Commoner, his job as Secretary was another failure. As war waged in Europe, he worked hard but unsuccessfully for peace. When it looked more and more as if Wilson was pushing America toward war, Bryan resigned his cabinet post in protest.

But if Bryan's life was well laced with failures, it also had its successes. He had helped, certainly, in gaining women the right to vote. He also helped in making alcoholic beverages illegal. And now there could be no doubt that he was helping the cause of fundamentalism.

The fundamentalists needed help, too, for they had picked a fight with a large and increasingly powerful group—the scientists of the world. The scientific world had arrived at the notion that man was not fashioned out of dust one day by God. His beginnings may have been as simple. But man's creation must have taken many days—in fact, millions if not billions of years. To the fundamentalists such a view was sinful.

The idea that man was the product of many years of gradual evolution was hardly a new and revolutionary idea in 1925. But there were certainly people still living who could remember when Charles Darwin first presented the idea to the public in 1859 in a book called *The Origin of Species.*

Just when the notion of evolution began is hard to decide. Some feel that Darwin's grandfather, Erasmus Darwin, might have been the first to plant the seed of the idea in the scientific community. But wherever the idea began, all agree that Charles Darwin should get most of the credit for making the notion seem reasonable.

Darwin's ideas on evolution began to form many years before he made them public in 1859. They are usually traced to a five-year sea voyage he started in 1831. The captain of the sailing ship *Beagle,* charged with surveying parts of the coast of South America and the nearby islands, took Darwin along to study the plants and animals of that little-known continent. What Darwin saw gradually convinced him that all living things must evolve over the years.

He found some of his best evidence on the Galapagos Islands. While the captain and crew of the *Beagle* spent five weeks charting this handful of small tropical islands lying west of Ecuador, Darwin studied their unusual plants and animals. He found some remarkable collections.

Perhaps the finches were the most remarkable. Thirteen different species of finches lived on the islands. Although they resembled the seed-eating birds that Darwin was familiar with, they all showed some differences in appearance. The differences in appearance often went along with differences in habits.

Like the more common finches, many of the Galapagos finches were seed eaters, though most also ate some insects, as finches often do. But some were insect eaters who had little use of seeds. And one kind ate only insects.

The differences in eating habits were often reflected in a difference in beak. The insect-eating finch had a slender beak like the insect-eating warbler's, a beak that would be useful for digging out larvae or worms but not for cracking seeds. The seed-eating finches all had blunt, heavy beaks that were useful for breaking hard shells or husks.

In later years as he worried about the many finches of the Galapagos, Darwin found he couldn't believe that each of the thirteen species had been created separately, as the Bible seemed to say. It would make much better sense if they had all evolved from some one kind of finch that had found its way to the Galapagos at some time in the distant past. For God to have placed thirteen kinds of finches on this small, remote collection of islands was hard for him to accept. It was easier, he decided, to accept evolution.

But how did the various Galapagos finches happen to evolve in different directions? Darwin decided it was all a matter of selection. Breeders of animals or plants had already shown that large changes can be made over the years by selection of just certain ones for breeding. And nature, Darwin decided, could also change animals or plants by selection. He called the process "natural selection."

Of course the selections of nature are not planned. They happen by chance. But chance favors the animals or plants that are better suited to their environment—"survival of the fittest," Darwin called it. In a population of finches that live in a region where insects are more available than seeds, the finches that are best equipped to eat insects will be the most likely to survive. And so any finch that happens to be born with a good beak for eating insects has a good chance of passing such a beak on to future finches.

It isn't too hard to see how seed-eating finches might evolve into insect-eating finches in such a way. That is a rather small change. But could finches possibly evolve enough to become robins, or eagles—or even animals that aren't birds?

In Darwin's mind it was all a matter of time. If an animal species can change a little in a hundred years, it could change a million times that much in a hundred million years. And that could be a lot. It might even be enough to change a monkey into a man.

In 1859 Darwin was careful not to discuss the ancient relatives of man. But his message was clear. When he suggested in *The Origin of Species* "that probably all the organic beings which have ever lived on this earth have descended from some one primordial form, into which life was first breathed," he clearly was talking about the remarkable human being as well as the beasts of field and forest—about man as well as mouse. If his message wasn't clear in 1859, he made it so in 1871, when he published *The Descent of Man.*

Darwin's ideas about the origin of man weren't accepted at once by all scientists. Some of them were quick to become "evolutionists," but some hesitated. In the 66 years since the publication of *The Origin of Species,* though, the picture had changed. So much new evidence had been found and so many gaps in Darwin's argument had been filled, that by 1925 it would have been hard to find a scientist anywhere who did not feel that man must have evolved from "lower" forms of life.

But of course it was a different matter with the fundamentalists. The theory of evolution and the Bible simply didn't agree, they felt. And since the Bible was the word of God, the theory must be wrong.

Feeling as they did, the fundamentalists were disturbed when they saw the theory of evolution being taught in the public schools. In the home and the church their children were taught that the words of the Bible were the gospel truth. But then they went to the school and were taught that they weren't. The truth about the origin of man, according to the schools, was to be found in the words of Darwin, not in the words of the Bible. To earnest fundamentalists this state of affairs was not only regrettable. It was something they must devote all their energy to changing.

One of the early tries at rooting evolution out of the public schools was made in Tennessee's neighboring state of Kentucky. In 1922, while Scopes labored at the University of Kentucky, Bryan came to the state to try to convince the legislature that teaching evolution should be outlawed in any public school in Kentucky—including the University. Mostly because of the strong outcry from the University, Bryan failed in his mission. But the vote in the legislature was very close.

The next year in Florida, Bryan had better success. Bryan had moved to Miami in 1921. In 1923 he managed to convince his new home state to go on record against evolution. The Florida legislature passed a resolution stating that it was "improper and subversive" to teach any idea "that links man in a blood relationship to any other form of life." The legislature didn't label such teaching an out-and-out crime. There was no announced penalty. It was simply pointed out that it was not the right thing for a teacher to do.

But then came Tennessee, where in 1925 the teaching of the theory of evolution was made a crime. It wasn't Bryan's doing, actually, though his influence couldn't be doubted. John Washington Butler, a part-time farmer, part-time schoolteacher, had argued during his campaign for the legislature that Tennessee needed a law against the teaching of evolution. When he won the election, he decided he had better write one. With no loud voices raised against Butler's antievolution bill, it quietly became the law of Tennessee. And so in Tennessee, talking about evolution became a crime—inside school, at least. And in the quiet town of Dayton a likeable young athletics coach named John Thomas Scopes became a criminal.

CHAPTER FOUR
THE GREAT
COMMONER
AND THE GREAT
DEFENDER

BRYAN CALLS SCIENTISTS DISHONEST SCOUNDRELS. Those harsh words headlined a New York *Times* report of Bryan's speech on May 13 before the third annual conference of the Sure Foundation Reformed Episcopalians, Lutherans, and Goshen Baptists of West Chester, Pennsylvania. The scientists of America, Bryan had told his fundamentalist audience, are "dishonest scoundrels, afraid to tell their beliefs, burrowing in the ground and stealing away the faith of your children."

In that May 13 talk Bryan was on an old subject. But he had found a new reason for talking about it. For the "dishonest scoundrels" had at last been forced to show themselves above ground. "We've got them now where they've got to come up and fight," gloated Bryan. "In Tennessee there is a law they can't teach man is descended from any lower form of life. Now that law has deliberately been violated."

Bryan announced that he would happily help punish the violator: "The fundamentalists are so interested in the case that I said I'd be one of their counsel if the law department of the state of Tennessee doesn't object."

The question raised in Tennessee, Bryan argued, was simply a matter of who should have the say in the education of children. "It is one of the greatest questions ever raised," he suggested—"the question of the right of the people who created and support the schools to control them. If not they, then who?"

The idea that a handful of scientists could dictate what was taught in science courses was preposterous to Bryan. "There are only 11,000 members of the American Association for the Advancement of Science," he pointed out. "I don't believe one in 10,000 should dictate to the rest of us. Can a handful of scientists rob your children of religion and turn them out atheists? We'll find 109 million of the other side." Then he added with a smirk: "For the first time in my life I'm on the side of the majority."

Bryan's offer to help the prosecution of the case against John Scopes was quickly accepted. Of course Bryan wasn't much of a lawyer. He hadn't practiced law in many years. He had been too busy being a writer and a talker since he had become interested in politics and now religion.

But to many of the people of Tennessee, including some of the lawyers who would prosecute it, the Scopes case was not just an argument between lawyers about whether the Butler Act was constitutional. This was a chance to put science in its place. And who could do that better than William Jennings Bryan? And who, the boosters of Dayton might add, could better draw attention to their beautiful little town in the hills of Tennessee?

But were even the boosters ready for what happened

next? According to one of the laws of motion, any action gives an equal and opposite reaction. That law wasn't intended to apply to human affairs, but Bryan's action seemed to fit it. As soon as the prosecution got the offer of help from the great William Jennings Bryan, the defense got an offer of help from the great Clarence Seward Darrow.

If Bryan was the best-known champion of fundamentalism, Clarence Darrow was its best-known foe. When he learned of Bryan's offer, he was delighted to counter with his own. Two days after Bryan's West Chester speech, Darrow sent a wire to Dayton that ended: ". . . in case you should need us, we are willing, without fees or expense, to help the defense of Professor Scopes in any way you may suggest or direct." The wire was also signed by Dudley Field Malone, a New York lawyer who had worked under Bryan when he was Secretary of State.

Clarence Darrow had earned a reputation as America's greatest criminal lawyer. In 1925 Darrow was 68 and doing less "lawyering" than he used to. But he was fresh from a triumph of a kind. In 1924 Nathan Leopold and Richard Loeb killed a boy in their wealthy Chicago neighborhood just to see what sort of thrill they would get from doing it. Their crime was discovered, and Darrow, who also lived in Chicago, defended them when they came to trial. There was no chance of saving Leopold and Loeb from conviction. But Darrow's brilliant arguments saved them from being executed for their crime. From that trial, if no other, Darrow became a national figure.

Darrow had tried to lock horns with Bryan over religion two years before. In the summer of 1923 Bryan had sent to the Chicago *Tribune* a questionnaire for professors who claimed to be evolutionists and Christians at the same time. Bryan, of course, didn't see how that was possible.

That questionnaire gave Darrow his chance. Darrow was an agnostic—a person who felt that the existence of a God has never been proved. He was also a strong supporter of science. Darrow sent off a letter to the *Tribune* with a questionnaire of his own. He agreed that a questionnaire for the professors might be a good way to make the issues clearer. But he also thought another questionnaire was needed: "A few questions to Mr. Bryan and the fundamentalists, if fairly answered, might serve the interest of reaching the truth." He added: "All of this assumes that truth is desirable." With the letter Darrow enclosed a list of 55 questions about the Bible—questions about the age of the earth, the origin of man, and so on.

Bryan, though, ignored Darrow's letter. He wasn't interested then in matching wits with Darrow. And perhaps two years later he would still have declined if the choice were his. But in 1925 he would find himself in the same courtroom with his questioner.

Darrow's offer to defend Scopes wasn't accepted right away. The services of the nation's foremost defender would seem an offer that the American Civil Liberties Union couldn't very well turn down. But they nearly did. The ACLU had hoped that this would be a sober trial to decide whether a state had the right to prevent a teacher from teaching what had been thought and written by the world's greatest scientists. But if Darrow's offer was accepted, the trial could easily become a circus. With the country's best-known fundamentalist on one side and the country's best-known agnostic on the other, the contest might come to be billed as Bryan versus Darrow, or the Bible versus *The Origin of Species,* instead of the State of Tennessee versus John Thomas Scopes. The issue, felt the ACLU, was not whether Bryan could outtalk Darrow, or whether the biblical story of creation was more reasonable than the theory of evolution. The issue was whether Tennessee could prevent John Scopes from telling his students what some of the leading thinkers of the world were thinking.

But it was the defendant himself who got the ACLU to accept Darrow's offer. Scopes had met with members of the ACLU and a few others in New York City to discuss his defense. As the arguments against accepting Darrow's offer were piled higher, the director of the ACLU turned to Scopes and said: "I think the defendant should be heard."

"I want Darrow," said Scopes in his soft Southern drawl, and he went on to explain that it was too late to stop the circus. The circus had already come to Dayton. With Bryan slated to bring his crusade against evolution to town, Dayton was already filling with "screwballs, con men, and devotees," as Scopes put it.

The members of the ACLU were still unconvinced. One of them wanted to accept the offer of Dudley Field Malone, who had also signed the telegram, and let Darrow's offer go. But Malone was at the meeting and would have none of that. Malone, a fashionable lawyer with a thriving divorce practice in New York and Paris, was sometimes described as a loudmouthed Irishman. He angrily told them that he wouldn't help at all unless Darrow was accepted. With Scopes and Malone both on his side, Darrow finally made it.

It was then early June. The trial had been scheduled for July 10. That gave Scopes a month to relax before his day in court—or so he thought.

CHAPTER FIVE
MONKEY BUSINESS

Scopes hadn't been home in Paducah long before he got a call from Dayton. It was Doc Robinson: "John, you have to come down here. There has been a shooting and there is a lot of other trouble developing."

"A shooting?" Scopes was amazed.

"I'm afraid so," said the druggist, and he didn't seem to be kidding.

"Anyone I know?" asked Scopes.

"Well, nobody has been hurt yet that I know of, but it could be a pretty bad situation."

With some vague sense of being responsible for what was going on, Scopes took the next train for Dayton. When he reached the once-sleepy town, he found it "had heated up considerably" since he had last seen it. But it hadn't really come to the point of people shooting at each other. The shooting was a fake.

It must have been a rather good fake, though, for it was reported in several newspapers. Two men had been arguing about evolution or maybe the Bible in the local barbershop, which was one of Dayton's popular hangouts. One of the men had pulled a gun in his anger and as the other man took flight, he chased after him, yelling oaths and blasting away with his pistol—loaded with blanks.

Scopes guessed who might have directed this little publicity stunt. It looked as if George Rappleyea, who had started the ball rolling, was trying to give it another shove. But Scopes decided he was going too far. Suppose some of the "screwballs" in town should be inspired by such stunts to use real bullets to settle their differences.

"There's been a shooting," Doc Robinson informed Scopes, *"and there is a lot of other trouble developing."*

George Rappleyea's interest in the case always puzzled Scopes. It was Rappleyea who had first suggested that Dayton try to get a test case of the Butler Act. In fact, it was Rappleyea who suggested that his friend Scopes could play the part of the criminal. "I didn't see how he could gain by the trial," said Scopes. But then he added: "At the same time, I knew him well enough to realize he wouldn't have done the things he did if he hadn't had an angle." Perhaps he thought the publicity might help his faltering mining business.

But Rappleyea had another reason that might have been more important. Some time before, Rappleyea had gone to a funeral for a boy killed in an accident. The minister, a fundamentalist, told the grieving mother that her son was now burning in the fires of Hell because he had never been baptized. Rappleyea was so shocked by the minister's cruel words that he then and there declared a private war on fundamentalism.

Rappleyea's biggest success at publicizing the approaching trial came when he tried to drag the well-known English writer H. G. Wells into the battle. Rappleyea mentioned to a newspaperman that Wells would be asked to aid Scopes's defense. Since Wells was best known for writing science-fiction, he would seem a strange ally. But the story was carried by the news services, and Wells was approached by reporters in England. He had never heard of John Scopes, he announced, nor of Dayton, Tennessee.

But with his reply, of course, everyone thereabout learned of Scopes and Dayton. Suddenly all England was interested in the trial of an obscure schoolteacher in an obscure American village. One of England's most famous residents, George Bernard Shaw, even wrote an article about the coming trial. *Where Darwin Is Taboo,* he called the article, which appeared shortly before the trial began. "It is not often that a single State can make a whole Continent ridiculous, or a single man set Europe asking whether America has ever really been civilised," he began. "But Tennessee and Mr. Bryan have brought off the double event." Having disposed of Bryan, Shaw later took a shot at the writer of the antievolution law: "Tennessee and Mr. Butler have had a nasty jolt. They have come up against a modern idea. Not a new idea, of course; only the idea of Evolution."

But unaware of the cutting comments that were being sharpened in the several corners of the world, Dayton was having fun getting ready for "the monkey business," as they called the coming trial. You could buy a button suggesting "Your Old Man's a Monkey" and wear it as you sipped your Monkey Fizz at Robinson's Drugstore. J. R. Darwin, who ran a clothing store, put up a large sign announcing "DARWIN IS RIGHT—Inside."

As the town readied itself for the big show, the defense did its best to keep it from happening—at least in Dayton. The lawyers of the ACLU felt that the law that Scopes had broken violated the Federal constitution as well as the State constitution. And so a few days before the date of the Dayton trial, Darrow and the other lawyers who would defend Scopes went to Cookeville, Tennessee, to see if they could put the case into the Federal court immediately without wasting time and money on the State trial.

It took the Cookeville judge little more than an hour to hear what they had to say and then to reject the plea. It appeared that the judge didn't want to spoil the fun. It also appeared that Darrow wasn't exactly dismayed by the ruling. Scopes later remarked: "Darrow, although he had done all he could to obtain a Federal injunction, seemed very pleased at Judge Gore's ruling. Now it would be easier to accomplish the goal for which he had first entered the case—to get Bryan."

Bryan came to town on July 7, three days before the trial was to start. A sizable part of Dayton went to the railway station to greet the Great Commoner. Their idol emerged from the train, which had made a special stop to let him off, wearing striped trousers and a dark wool jacket —not the best choice of garb for a Dayton summer day.

A few minutes later, though, Bryan had happily shed his jacket. As an automobile procession escorted him to his lodgings, he sat smiling in his shirt sleeves, a white pith helmet protecting his glistening bald head from the merciless Dayton sun.

Bryan's welcome was as warm in spirit as in temperature. Basking in the warmth of Dayton's admiration, he exclaimed as he reached his destination: "This is the day I've been waiting for!"

Scopes hadn't been at the station to see Bryan arrive, but he did see him that night. The Dayton Progressive Club gave Bryan a banquet and invited Scopes.

William Jennings Bryan's arrival in Dayton brought a more serious note to the carnival atmosphere of the town.

After the banquet had been opened with a prayer, Scopes found himself sitting opposite the honored guest at the head table. Just as at his high-school graduation, he would have a ringside seat for the inevitable speech that would follow the meal. Much to his surprise, Bryan reminded him of that earlier speech.

"John, I know you," said Bryan, leaning across the table. His manner was pleasant as he recalled what must have been an unpleasant moment: "I think you're one of those high-school students who made a disturbance at that commencement address I delivered in Salem several years ago!"

Scopes blushed and admitted he was one of the culprits. Bryan laughed. He seemed anxious to stay on friendly terms. When Scopes assured him that he respected him in spite of their difference of opinion, Bryan was pleased. "Good," he said to his young foe. "We shall get along fine."

Bryan's talk that night was a friendly, folksy sort of speech. But he did get serious at one point. "The contest between evolution and Christianity," he proclaimed dramatically, "is a duel to the death!" The phrase rang like a battle cry. "If evolution wins in Dayton," he continued, "Christianity goes." To fundamentalist Bryan there could be no compromise: "They are as antagonistic as light and darkness, as good and evil!"

With Bryan's coming, Dayton changed its tune. Bryan didn't come to town to joke about evolution. This was a serious matter. And Dayton became more serious. The monkey signs came down and religious signs went up. The largest of them was a huge banner saying, READ YOUR BIBLE DAILY.

Dayton had attracted all kinds of people. Mountaineers carrying squirrel guns wandered into town to see what was going on. Reporters by the dozen arrived to describe the scene and the coming trial. But probably the most noticeable newcomers were the preachers and would-be preachers from various fundamentalist organizations. Speeches could be heard on any street corner, and tents sprouted here and there to house revival meetings. Any evolutionist wanting to be "saved" didn't have far to go to find salvation.

Journalist H. L. Mencken, in fact, reported that he was "converted" at a camp meeting of the Holy Rollers, then "saved" several times by the secretary of the Anti-Evolution League. Mencken, though, wasn't really seeking salvation. He was seeking stories for the Baltimore *Evening Sun.*

H. L. Mencken was already becoming famous for his biting wit. He had developed a great talent for poking fun. It was Mencken who christened the case against John Thomas Scopes, the Monkey Trial. And his columns about the trial delighted—or infuriated—more than his Baltimore audience. He was well read in Dayton, for his column was reprinted in the Chattanooga *News.* And the local readers were more often "infuriated."

But Mencken had some nice things to say about Dayton, though even his compliments often sounded like insults: "The town, I confess, greatly surprised me. I expected to find a squalid Southern village, with darkies snoozing on the horseblocks, pigs rooting under the houses and the inhabitants full of hookworm and malaria. What I found was a country town full of charm and even beauty."

As the audience of reporters and mountaineers and "screwballs" assembled in this charming, beautiful country town of Dayton, so did the cast of characters who would act out the courtroom drama. Though Bryan was the big name of the prosecution, he had a large supporting cast.

Tom Stewart, the attorney general, was to be in charge. Stewart was a young, able lawyer who took his job seriously—in fact he seemed to take all of life seriously. Tall and dark, his most frequent expression seemed to be a frown.

Four other Tennesseans would assist the prosecution: Ben McKenzie and his son Gordon, and the Hicks brothers, Sue and Herbert. Finally, Bryan's own son from distant Los Angeles, William Jennings Bryan, Jr., rounded out the prosecution. It was a much related crew.

The defense team was also trickling into town. Darrow had stayed behind in Cookeville and so had missed Bryan's banquet. But he got to town the next day and was given a banquet himself. The Dayton Progressive Club apparently decided that the defense should get equal time.

Agnostic or not, the Daytonians couldn't help but like the easygoing and humorous Darrow. At one point in his talk after the dinner, he described how he got established as a lawyer. "For a while I was practicing law and playing poker on the side," he said, "and I almost starved." The coming punch line was obvious, but the audience enjoyed it: "But then I started playing poker and practicing law on the side, and I made enough money to go to Chicago and open an office!"

The defense team was also a fair-sized group. Besides Darrow and Malone, the ACLU had sent Arthur Garfield Hays from their own staff. These three "foreigners" were joined by a Tennessean, John Neal. Neal was no stranger to the ways of the fundamentalists. He had been fired from the University of Tennessee two years before for supporting an evolutionist on the faculty. When Scopes was arrested for teaching about evolution, Neal came quickly to Dayton to offer his services. Besides these four, who carried almost all the argument in court, several others helped out. All counted, the defense were almost as numerous as the prosecution.

To direct these opposing casts of characters in the drama that was about to begin, there came to Dayton a native of the mountain town of Gizzards Cove, Tennessee —Judge John T. Raulston. "Ruddy, genial, sunburnt, smooth shaven," one reporter described him. Half lawyer, half politician, he made a good master of ceremonies for the coming show. When he came to town, he pleased everyone by announcing, as he fanned himself with his straw hat, that "coats off" would be the rule in his courtroom.

And so on a hot Thursday evening in July the little town of Dayton, Tennessee, now bulging with visitors, went to sleep with the prospect of beginning "the world's most famous trial" in the morning. If it didn't turn out to be the most famous, it would surprise everyone. It was hard to imagine, at least, that any trial could have a bigger build-up.

CHAPTER SIX
A JURY
OF HIS PEERS

Oh, God, our divine father, we recognize thee as the supreme ruler of the universe, in whose hands are the lives and destinies of all men, and of all the world."

It was 9 o'clock on Friday, the 10th of July, 1925, and the Reverend Cartwright was opening the first day of the trial of John Thomas Scopes. The summer sun had been shining on the Dayton courthouse for nearly four and a half hours by then, and the second-floor courtroom was already getting uncomfortably warm. Dudley Field Malone, his double-breasted jacket buttoned, seemed not to notice the heat. But Clarence Darrow, although a white necktie still circled his neck, had long since shed his coat to expose a pair of blue suspenders.

"We pray that the power and the presence of the Holy Spirit may be with the jury and with the accused and with all the attorneys." As the prayer went on and on, threatening to become a sermon, many in the large audience responded with amens at appropriate moments. Bryan, also in shirtsleeves, sat with his eyes lowered and his palm-leaf fan stilled for the time being.

"It was incredible," Scopes later wrote, "that I was the central figure on this stage." Scopes had also taken notice of the weather. His coat was off, his shirt open at the neck, and his sleeves rolled up. He sat between the two men who probably had the most to do with getting him into all this —his father and George Rappleyea.

The courtroom had begun to fill two hours before. The large grounds were ringed with automobiles and buggies. Horses were tied here and there, dripping saliva and shaking flies from their glistening flanks. A long-handled pump standing near the entrance of the courthouse had been kept busy providing water for the animals.

As the courtroom had filled, the hum of conversation had increased, threatening to drown the clatter of the reporters' typewriters and the fainter clicking of the telegraph instruments. Over a hundred reporters from all parts of the country sat at the press tables. Two reporters from London recorded the events for their British audience. Perhaps the most unlikely member of the press corps was John Washington Butler, author of the Butler Act, who had managed to get an assignment from a press association and so took his place among the veteran reporters.

Judge Raulston had announced that there would be no smoking while court was in session, and so some—including John Scopes—had used the moments before the trial began to have a cigarette.

Photographers were everywhere, some taking movies as the members of the cast arrived, others snapping stills in and out of the courtroom. Judge Raulston had posed with his gavel raised.

Bryan had entered shortly before nine to be greeted by a burst of applause. He crossed to shake hands with Darrow, who was already seated, and was cheered again. In the minds of most of the audience, there was no question about who was the star of this show.

"God help us to be loyal to God, and loyal to truth."
The prayer finally reached an ending and the judge called
the case: "State of Tennessee versus John Thomas
Scopes."

But if the prayer was over, the preliminaries were not.
In Tennessee, as in many states, a grand jury must first
decide whether the state has a reasonable case against the
defendant. A special grand jury had decided back on May
25 that the State of Tennessee did surely have a case
against John Scopes. But now there was some question
whether it had all been done in a proper manner. The
obvious solution was to do it over again.

The grand jury had already been selected. But Judge
Raulston had to instruct its members. That involved reading the Butler Act, of course. It also involved reading the
Bible. The thirty-one verses of the first chapter of Genesis,
the judge decided, would be enough. Actually, they didn't
mention man's creation from dust, but they did include
another story of man's creation by God. "And God said,
Let us make man in our image, after our likeness," intoned
Raulston, as he reached the crucial words of the 26th and
27th verses: "and let them have dominion over the fish of
the sea, and over the fowl of the air, and over the cattle,
and over all the earth, and over every creeping thing that
creepeth upon the earth. So God created man in his own
image, in the image of God created he him; male and
female created he them."

With the grand jury instructed, court adjourned for
about an hour while the jury met to hear testimony and

to reach a decision. Many of the audience spilled out onto the courthouse lawn. The drinking fountains that had been specially installed around the grounds attracted small crowds. As the sun had climbed, so had the temperature.

A gray-bearded mountaineer emerging from the courthouse exclaimed: "Didn't that blessed old Bible sound good as he read it to the grand jury!"

A blind musician was stationed on the courthouse lawn playing a hand organ. As he began playing old-fashioned hymns, a crowd gathered and joined in with singing.

Scopes spent part of the intermission with the grand jury. One of the students who was supposed to testify didn't want to say anything against his teacher. The grand jury had to send for Scopes to tell the boy that it was all right. With Scopes's help, the grand jury completed their investigation on schedule and decided that the State should try Scopes for his crime.

By the time the court convened again, it was nearly time for lunch. Judge Raulston had set the court hours at 9 to 4:30 with a two-hour break beginning at 11:30.

At the noon recess most of the locals headed home for lunch. But the hundreds of visitors found food and drink close by. Lemonade stands, barbecue stands, and various other temporary sources of refreshment that ringed the courthouse grounds did a brisk business. A pit fifty feet long and four feet wide had been dug in the courthouse lawn for the barbecuing. Some of the visitors spread their own picnic meals under the trees that partially shaded the courthouse lawn. There was a holiday atmosphere as people clustered in small groups here and there chattering and laughing.

But John Scopes was back in the courtroom early after the lunch break and sat reading a newspaper. His father sat beside him, looking bored and stirring up the hot, humid air with a fan.

The afternoon session was spent in selecting a jury for the trial. The grand jury had decided that Scopes should be tried. Now a new collection of citizens was needed to decide his guilt or innocence.

A sandy-haired boy of two sat on the judge's desk and drew names for the jury from a hat. Each possible juror was interviewed first by the judge, then by Attorney General Stewart, then by Darrow.

Darrow asked most of the questions. After he found what a prospective juror did for a living and what church he belonged to, Darrow usually quizzed him about evolution.

"Do you know anything about evolution?" Darrow asked the third prospective juror, Jim Riley.

"No, not particularly," answered Riley.

"Heard about it?"

"Yes, I've heard about it."

"Know what it is?"

"I don't know much about it," admitted Riley.

Darrow then went on to find if he had formed an opinion about evolution: "Ever heard anyone preach any sermons on it?"

"Do you know anything about evolution?" Clarence Darrow asked prospective juror Jim Riley.

"No, sir," answered Riley.

"Ever hear Mr. Bryan speak about it?"

"No, sir."

"Ever read anything he said about it?"

"No, sir," said Riley. Then he added: "I can't read."

"Well," said Darrow with a smile, "you are fortunate."

Jim Riley was accepted as a juror. But J. R. Massingill, who followed him, didn't make it. After Darrow discovered he was a preacher, he asked him: "Did you ever preach on evolution?"

"Yes," answered Massingill. "I haven't as a subject. Just taken that up in connection with other subjects. I have referred to it in discussing them."

"Against it or for it?"

"I'm strictly for the Bible," said Massingill.

"I am talking about evolution. I am not talking about the Bible," said Darrow. "Did you preach for or against evolution?"

Massingill squirmed. He clearly wanted to get on that jury: "Is that a fair question, Judge?"

"Yes," said Judge Raulston. "Answer the question."

"Well," admitted Massingill, "I preached against it, of course."

The audience in the courtroom burst into applause. Frowning, Darrow objected to the improper audience participation. In the end, he also objected to Massingill, who was then excused from being a juror.

By the middle of the afternoon the necessary twelve men had been selected. They were mostly farmers, and

even those that weren't had some tie with the soil. Nine of them were full-time farmers, one was a teacher who farmed part-time, one was a farm owner, and one was a shipping clerk who did a little farming on the side.

Eleven of the twelve were church members, which in those parts usually meant they were fundamentalists. As H. L. Mencken reported to the readers of the Baltimore *Evening Sun:* "It was obvious after a few rounds that the jury would be unanimously hot for Genesis. The most that Mr. Darrow could hope for was to sneak in a few men bold enough to declare publicly that they would have to hear the evidence against Scopes before condemning him."

The jury selection had gone on "in the atmosphere of a blast furnace," as Mencken put it, and Judge Raulston took the first chance to adjourn. With the jury chosen, the trial could now begin in earnest—but on Monday.

As the jury filed out of the courtroom, somebody noted that there were "three coat-wearing dudes in the dozen." Thomas Scopes was standing outside the courtroom with a reporter as the jury passed. "Now, Dad," warned John, who knew his father only too well, "don't you go talking to that reporter."

But his dad was bound to speak his piece. "Say, brother," he whispered to the reporter, "that's a hell of a jury!"

CHAPTER SEVEN
A FLOURISH
OF BUGLES

With over a hundred reporters in town to cover the trial, something had to happen on the weekend, even if the reporters had to invent it.

Saturday night Scopes went to the usual Saturday-night dance given by a hotel in the nearby resort town of Morgan Springs, as he had often done before. With so many drawn to the Dayton area by the trial, both the hotel and the separate dance pavillion were jammed.

Scopes behaved like the young, unmarried teacher he was, dancing with Dayton girls he knew. But then one of his partners, a model of innocence, mentioned that she needed to walk to the hotel but was afraid to walk alone through the unlighted area between the pavillion and the hotel. Without thinking anything strange in her request, Scopes agreed to go with her.

"As we were walking in the darkness," Scopes later reported, "she suddenly wrapped her arms around my neck and started kissing me. She caught me totally by surprise and as I stood there, momentarily paralyzed, floodlights flashed on." Scopes, it appeared, had been set up to give some lurking reporter a news picture.

Others in the trial made minor news, too. On Saturday, Darrow and Bryan both had statements to make. Then on Sunday Bryan managed to deliver two sermons—one at a Methodist Episcopal church and another on the court-house lawn, where a speaking platform had been erected.

Bryan hadn't uttered a word inside the courthouse. But he was making up for it outside.

The court session on Monday started much as Friday's session had started—hot and prayerful. All the seats of the courtroom were again full, with several hundred people standing around the outskirts of the room.

"There were three new objects," wrote one reporter. Microphones had been installed by the Chicago radio station WGN to carry the sound of the proceedings to the nation—or at least to those people who had radio sets that would pick up the Chicago station. It would be the first time a trial had been broadcast. Speakers were also installed outside the courthouse to keep those who couldn't squeeze into the courtroom in touch with what was going on.

Although Dudley Field Malone still kept his double-breasted jacket buttoned, most of the principals had yielded to the continuing heat. Judge Raulston had changed from his blue woolen suit of Friday to a cooler one of linen. Clarence Darrow, as usual, had removed his coat, revealing a pair of scarlet suspenders. William Jennings Bryan had shed not only his coat but half his shirt. From its formal stripes and starched front, it was evident that his shirt once carried starched collar and cuffs. But now it sported a comfortable collarless V neck and short sleeves. The defendant John Scopes, also without coat and tie, sat puffing a cigarette as he waited for court to open.

When the session got under way, Attorney General Tom Stewart read the indictment. "State of Tennessee,

County of Rhea, Circuit Court, July Special Term, 1925," he droned. "The grand jurors for the state aforesaid, being duly summoned, elected, empaneled, sworn and charged to inquire for the body of the county aforesaid . . ." The indictment followed the familiar wording of the Butler Act in defining Scopes's crime. But it did introduce one new item of interest. His crime, it charged, had occurred on the 24th day of April. Although the indictment didn't say so, the date—just one week before school let out—was really just a guess.

When Stewart had completed the formality of reading the indictment, Judge Raulston performed another formality. Turning to the defense team, he asked: "What is your plea, gentlemen?"

But as the judge well knew, it wasn't time yet for the plea. The question of Scopes's guilt or innocence would have to wait. The law must go on trial first. "May it please your honor," spoke up Tennessean John Neal, "we make a motion to quash the indictment . . ."

In plain language, Neal might have said: "We ask you to drop the charges." The legal word "quash" doesn't mean squash, but it comes close to it. To a lawyer it means cancel or overthrow. And there were a dozen reasons, the defense felt, why the charges against John Scopes should be overthrown—a baker's dozen, it turned out.

As John Neal began to state the thirteen legal arguments for quashing, the audience hardly paid him full attention. If they had been told that the motion to quash the indictment was the vital issue of the case, they would surely have been disappointed. It didn't sound very exciting.

Neal was not an impressive man. Scopes called him "a good man and a clear thinker." He would even write years later, "His coming to Dayton was one of the fortunate things that happened to me that summer." But Neal had a weak voice and a shy manner. On top of that, he was usually untidy and illshaven.

Most of the arguments for quashing the indictment were "lawyers' arguments"—arguments that would interest anybody whose business it was to worry about the fine points of the law, but hardly anyone else. The Butler Act, explained Neal, violated ten different articles of the constitution of Tennessee. And most of these were articles that no ordinary person had ever heard of or cared much about. Besides the ten violations of the Tennessee constitution, the defense had found three other arguments against the law, one based on the U.S. constitution.

Even at the best of times the audience in the Dayton courtroom didn't sit in rapt attention, for there were many distractions. "Dogs roam through the courtroom during the trial, sniffing about under the bench until someone sends them yelping out with well-directed boots . . ." reported one newsman. "Pop bottles are emptied whenever a spectator gets thirsty and the empty bottles go plopping on the floor at unexpected intervals. Babies are allowed in the courtroom and they wail unadmonished. Trains roar by every now and then." It was no stretch of the imagination to liken the courtroom scene to a circus, as Scopes would later do. Added the newsman: "Vendors hawk, 'Nice soft cushions, ten cents.' "

After Neal had stated the thirteen arguments, he went back and discussed them in turn. It was mostly a dreary performance. But buried among the technical points were two arguments that touched on fundamental freedoms. Two basic rights were violated by the Butler Act, argued Neal: freedom of religion and freedom of speech. Modeled after the U.S. constitution, the Tennessee constitution insisted that "no preference shall ever be given, by law, to any religious establishment or mode of worship." Yet the Butler Act gave special favor to the Bible and to any worship that rests upon it. Certainly, proposed Neal, it must violate that article.

The Tennessee constitution also followed the United States constitution in proclaiming freedom of speech. "The free communication of thoughts and opinions," it read, "is one of the invaluable rights of man, and every citizen may freely speak, write, and print on any subject . . ." Yet John Scopes, freely speaking of evolution, was arrested for his act. In the eyes of the defense, this article too was clearly violated by the antievolution law.

Slipped in between these two arguments, though, was a short interruption, courtesy of Attorney General Stewart. As Neal was about to begin his plea for freedom of speech, it suddenly occurred to Stewart that something was wrong here. What was the jury doing listening to all this? The jury would have no part in this decision. It was for the judge alone to rule whether the indictment should be quashed. And maybe the jury would be prejudiced by listening to all these arguments about whether the law was good or bad.

Darrow, of course, didn't agree. Any questions that were raised about the law would surely help the defense. He objected to the jury's retiring.

"You don't object?" asked Stewart, apparently misunderstanding.

"We do object," corrected Darrow.

"It don't make any difference whether you do or not," said the outspoken Stewart. And in the end it didn't. Whether the jury was present, it developed, was up to Judge Raulston. And the judge decided he would be "more at ease with the jury not present."

"We will be less at ease," said Darrow.

"Let the jury retire," said the judge.

After the twelve men who had been so pleased with their ringside seats gave them up, Neal finished his arguments and then gave Arthur Garfield Hays, the ACLU lawyer, a turn. Hays was a rugged individual with a rugged talent. Scopes called him "our key legal expert." Well dressed but more casual than his fellow New Yorker Malone, Hays was described as "thickset, stocky, democratic-looking, with rough shirt, open at the neck." His "rough shirt," complained Hays, came from the same expensive shop that sold dapper Malone his "well-fitting Metropolitan shirts."

Hays livened the proceedings a little by presenting a law against the teaching of modern astronomy. If a law against teaching about evolution is constitutional, argued Hays, then a law against teaching about the solar system would also be constitutional. "Be it enacted by the General Assembly of the State of Tennessee," he began, and then went on to recite a law that sounded just like the Butler Act except in a few places. It would be unlawful, the "Hays Act" said, "to teach any theory that denies the story that the earth is the center of the universe, as taught in the Bible, and to teach instead that the earth and planets move around the sun." Remembering that the Italian philosopher Giordano Bruno was burned at the stake in 1600 for such teaching, Hays wrote a stiff penalty into his act: "Any teacher found guilty . . . shall be put to death."

After Neal and Hays had had their say, the prosecution took their turn. Two "generals" carried most of the argument: General Ben McKenzie and General Tom Stewart. Tennesseans were great for titles. The defendant was often addressed as Professor Scopes. And even the "foreigner" from Chicago had become Colonel Darrow. McKenzie had earned his title of General by once being assistant attorney general. And naturally Attorney General Stewart had to be addressed as General too, though the title didn't seem to fit him so well.

General Ben McKenzie was usually described as "rotund." And his pink, round face was always in a chuckle. The general had one thing in common with Darrow, he had pointed out in court on Friday. The general and the colonel were both "suspender men." Like Darrow, McKenzie was also attuned to the humorous in life.

McKenzie, in his short speech, managed to rile the defense—Malone, especially—by his sarcastic references to their points of origin. As he spoke of "the great metropolitan city of New York," he was obviously not seeking to praise it. Nor was his allusion to Chicago as "the great white city of the northwest" intended as a compliment. Malone finally rose to object. "I do not consider further allusion to geographical parts of the country as particularly necessary," said Malone, "such as reference to New Yorkers and citizens of Illinois. We are here rightfully as American citizens."

Judge Raulston tried to calm the fiery Malone. "Colonel Malone, you do not know General McKenzie as well as the court does," said Raulston. "Everything he says is in a good humor."

But then the judge in trying further to soothe Malone made matters worse: "I want you gentlemen from New York or any other foreign state to always remember that you are our guests," he purred, "and that we accord you the same privileges and rights and courtesies that we do any other lawyer."

"Your Honor, we want to have it understood we deeply appreciate the hospitality of the court and the people of Tennessee, and the courtesies that are being extended to us at this time," answered Malone, almost amiably. Then he drew a sharp distinction: "But we want it understood that while we are in this courtroom we are here as lawyers, not as guests!"

When Malone had retreated, McKenzie began again.

"Your Honor," said McKenzie in his thick Southern drawl, "we have the very highest regard for these distinguished lawyers." But then he added: "I will admit that I have no respect for their opinions . . ."

Sue Hicks finished off the morning with a few odds and ends of arguments. Hicks owed his unusual first name to having had a mother who died during his birth. His grieving father named the newborn child after the departed mother.

During the midday recess Scopes showed some of the newsmen one way to fight the Dayton heat. A tributary of the Tennessee River ran past Dayton, forming a pool just right for swimming. Scopes took some of the wilted reporters down to the pool for a cooling dip. In keeping with the climate, an abandoned furnace served as a dressing room.

When court reconvened, the other general took his turn at showing how foolish were the arguments of the defense. Take the issue of freedom of religion. How could the Butler Act possibly interfere with religious worship? "You can attend the public schools of this state and go to any church you please," insisted General Stewart.

As for freedom of speech, the Butler Act surely didn't interfere with that either. "Mr. Scopes might have taken his stand on the street corners and expounded until he became hoarse as a result of his effort," said Stewart, "and we could not interfere with him." John Scopes on a street corner would be quite free to talk evolution to anybody who would listen. "But," added Stewart, "he cannot go into the public schools or a schoolhouse which is controlled by the legislature and supported by public funds of the State and teach this theory." What John Scopes may teach in a school that is supported by the State is a matter for the State to decide. And the State had decided he may not teach anything about evolution. It was as simple as that.

By the rules of Tennessee, the defense had the right to speak last on the motion. Now that the prosecution had probably convinced Judge Raulston that there was no earthly reason for quashing the indictment, the defense had a last chance to unconvince him. And the defense had saved its biggest gun for that job—Clarence Darrow.

As Darrow rose to address the judge, he hooked his thumbs under his suspenders and began in a chatty manner. Darrow had no great reputation as a silver-tongued orator. He was no Bryan. But he knew how to talk to a man, and he quickly got the full attention of Judge Raulston, and with it the attention of everybody in the courtroom.

Darrow had some nice things to say about the treatment Tennessee was giving him: "I shall always remember that this court is the first one that ever gave me the great title of Colonel." But it soon became obvious that he had some harsh things to say too. He had no intention of hiding how he felt about the Butler Act and the people behind it.

Darrow took his cue from the prosecution. The local prosecution lawyers had often reminded the court that the defense lawyers were mostly "foreigners." Darrow now used the General's taunting as an excuse to bring Bryan into his remarks. "So far as coming from other cities is concerned," he said pleasantly, "why, your honor, it is easy here. I came from Chicago, and my friend Malone and friend Hays came from New York." But there were several other "foreigners" involved, too, he wished to point out. "And on the other side we have a distinguished and very pleasant gentleman from California," he continued, referring to Bryan's son. And then he released his first blast at the Great Commoner: "And another who is prosecuting this case and who is responsible for this foolish, mischievous, and wicked act, who comes from Florida." Darrow wanted no one to doubt where he placed the blame for the Butler Act. John Washington Butler may have written it and the legislature of Tennessee may have passed it, but it was William Jennings Bryan who had inspired it.

Bryan sat silently without showing any emotion as Darrow recited again the evils and errors of the law. "Here we find today as brazen and as bold an attempt to destroy learning as was ever made in the Middle Ages. The only difference is we have not provided that they shall be burned at the stake." Then he added, only half in jest: "But there is time for that, your honor. We have to approach these things gradually."

Dead serious though he was, Darrow's sense of humor often showed through. As he spoke of the dangers of religious intolerance, he couldn't resist making fun of the Butler Act. "There is nothing else since man . . ." he had begun, but then he stopped. He snapped his scarlet suspenders. "I don't know whether I dare say 'evolved,' " he said. "Still, this isn't School!"

Darrow had started his remark with a jest, but he finished it with some harsh words about religion: "There is nothing else, your honor, that has caused the difference of opinion, the bitterness, the hatred, the war, the cruelty, that religion has caused." As the audience cringed, he added, softening his voice: "With that, of course, it has given consolation to millions."

Later, Darrow grew sarcastic as he ridiculed the fundamentalists who would use the Bible as a yardstick of learning. "Are your mathematics good?" he asked. "Turn to I Elijah 2." The references were phony, but they made his point. "Is your philosophy good? See II Samuel 3. Is your astronomy good? See Genesis, chapter 2, verse 7. Is your chemistry good? See—well, chemistry—see Deuteronomy 3:6 or anything that tells about brimstone."

Repeatedly Darrow pled for tolerance. To Darrow, mankind could not survive without tolerance for each other's beliefs and opinions. "If men are not tolerant, if men cannot respect each other's opinions, if men cannot live and let live, then no man's life is safe." Darrow thrust his head forward as he repeated the words: "No man's life is safe!"

"Here is a country," continued Darrow, "made up of Englishmen, Irishmen, Scotch, German—Europeans, Asiatics, Africans—men of every sort and men of every creed and men of every scientific belief. Who is going to

The citizens of Rhea County flocked to the trial just as they would to a circus.

begin this sorting out and say: 'I shall measure you . . .'? Where is that man wise enough to do it?"

Darrow's speech was designed for hearing. "You have but a dim notion of it," wrote reporter Mencken, "who have only read it." There was something about the way Darrow delivered his arguments—"the clang tint of it," Mencken called it—that made them more moving than they seem on paper.

In Mencken's words, Darrow's speech "rose like a wind and ended like a flourish of bugles." But the flourish almost didn't happen. "If today . . ." Darrow had begun, when Judge Raulston butted in: "Sorry to interrupt your argument, but it is adjourning time."

"If I may, I can close in five minutes . . ." said Darrow.

"Proceed tomorrow," said the judge.

But Darrow wasn't to be stopped: "If today you can take a thing like evolution and make it a crime to teach it in the public school, tomorrow you can make it a crime to teach it in the private schools. And the next year you can make it a crime to teach it in the hustings, or in the church. At the next session you may ban books and the newspapers."

One sleeve of Darrow's shirt had sprung a hole that widened each time he folded his arms. As Darrow continued, Raulston shifted in his seat. It was time for the bugles: "After a while, your honor, it is the setting of man against man and creed against creed until with flying banners and beating drums we are marching backward to the glorious ages of the sixteenth century when bigots lighted fagots to burn men who dared to bring any intelligence and enlightenment and culture to the human mind."

The "flourish of bugles" had sounded, and court promptly adjourned. Darrow had shown all doubters that he deserved his reputation, even if they didn't agree with him. General Ben McKenzie threw an arm around Darrow and said in a choked voice: "It was the greatest speech I ever heard in my life on any subject!"

Scopes, surveying the crowd as the session broke up, saw other evidence of approval. "Darrow had won the respect of the town when he spoke at the welcoming banquet several nights previously," he later wrote, "and now his opening speech in the trial made his reputation a firm one."

But reporter Mencken had a different reaction—perhaps because it suited his special writing talent better. He noted in his column the next day that "the morons in the audience, when it was over, simply hissed it." Of course he didn't say how many morons were in the audience. But he neatly wrapped up his low opinion of the listeners in a stinging sentence: "The net effect of Clarence Darrow's great speech yesterday seems to be precisely the same as if he had bawled it up a rainspout in the interior of Afghanistan."

CHAPTER EIGHT
PRAYER
AND PIRACY

On Monday night Dayton lost its electricity. At a street corner in the center of town, a preacher cried out: "The wrath of God has visited us!" Dayton was being punished, he decided, for permitting those evolutionists to speak against the Bible.

But it appeared more an act of man than of God. A man digging a ditch had accidentally sent his pick through a water main. Shutting off the water to repair the main meant shutting down the electric power plant too.

Monday night was also livened by the appearance of a monkey in Dayton—a real one. It was a young chimpanzee from a circus in Atlanta. Suited up like a man and carrying a cane, it drew a huge crowd as it paraded down Main street.

Tuesday morning Judge Raulston arrived in court looking "drowsy," one newsman reported. He was probably poorly prepared for what the newsman termed "a bombshell." But Clarence Darrow was prepared to drop one in the courtroom.

After the bailiff had rapped for order, Raulston made a very usual request: "Reverend Stribling, will you open with prayer." But he didn't get the usual response. Before Reverend Stribling could begin his entreaty to God, Darrow was asking for the judge's ear: "Your honor, I want to make an objection before the jury comes in."

"What is it, Mr. Darrow," asked Judge Raulston.

"I object to prayer and I object to the jury being present when the court rules on the objection."

Attorney General Stewart seemed unable to believe his ears. "What is it?" he asked.

"He objects to the court being opened with prayer," explained Judge Raulston, a pained look on his face, "especially in the presence of the jury."

The room began to buzz with reactions of the people in the audience. "If anything had come straight from heaven and had struck down the man who had uttered these words," reported one newsman, "it would not have surprised many in the courtroom."

Judge Raulston was not only shocked by Darrow's objection, he was clearly annoyed. "I believe I have a right," he whined. "I am responsible for the conduct of the court."

But Darrow had a different view of the matter: "The nature of this case being one where it is claimed by the State that there is a conflict between science and religion," argued Darrow, there should be "no attempt by means of prayer or any other way to influence the deliberation and consideration of the jury of the facts of the case."

Darrow's objection stirred up a lively argument. McKenzie and Stewart—the "generals"—each had something to say. And after Stewart had complained about the "idea extended by the agnostic counsel for the defense," Malone, too, joined the argument to show that a Christian member of the defense also objected to the daily prayer—which helps, he argued, "to increase the atmosphere of hostility to our point of view."

But in the end Judge Raulston overruled Darrow's objection and the daily plea for God's guidance was recited: "We pray, our father, to bless the proceedings of this court. Bless the court, the judge as he presides. And may there be in every heart and in every mind a reverence to the great creator of the world."

The first order of business, Judge Raulston had hoped, would be the reading of his decision on the motion to quash the indictment. And he had been up late trying to write it down. But with the power failure and all, he explained, he just didn't get it quite finished. He needed the rest of the morning. He adjourned the court until one o'clock.

As Scopes left the courthouse, he happened to run into William Hutchinson, a reporter for International News Service. Hutchinson, whom Scopes had gotten to know, suggested that the two have lunch together. That invitation made Scopes a spectator at what looked like a minor event. But what he witnessed caused a major upset in the course of the trial.

Hutchinson first wanted a word with Judge Raulston. The judge had left the courthouse ahead of them, and so they hurried to overtake him. After they had caught up, the reporter warmed the judge's heart by complimenting him on the efficient way he was handling the trial. Then he asked Raulston: "Are you going to render your decision on the constitutionality of the law when court convenes this afternoon?"

"That is my intention," said Raulston.

Then, referring to the next big issue that the judge would have to rule on, he asked Raulston: "Will the admissibility of the scientific testimony be the next order of business?"

"That is my understanding," said the judge, never realizing that his offhand answer tipped off Hutchinson to his decision. His answer could only mean that he was not quashing the indictment. For if he were quashing it, that would end the case. The question of scientific testimony wouldn't come up next—or ever.

"I thought Hutchinson was going to expose the trap he had set by running away too quickly," said Scopes, when he reported the incident. When Hutchinson finally managed to break free gracefully, he quickly sent the scoop to his news service.

The afternoon session didn't convene at one o'clock as planned. It was quarter past two before Judge Raulston appeared, and then only to postpone the session again. The judge was obviously disturbed. "I want to announce that I gave strict instructions to the stenographer that my opinion was not to be released to any person," he began. It was evident that some newsman had somehow gotten wind of his decision.

When court reconvened at quarter to four, the judge's decision on quashing was forgotten for a while. Hays wanted to present a petition about prayer.

Tom Stewart, though, had other ideas. "Your honor, just a minute," he sputtered. "I submit that it is absolutely out of order." Stewart felt that the judge's ruling on prayer during the morning session should have settled the matter.

But Hays didn't intend to give up easily. As Stewart took exception, he pressed to be heard: "I insist on making this motion!" The attorney general was just as insistent. "I am making my exception to the court," he snapped. "Will you please keep your mouth shut!"

Hays wasn't one to keep his mouth shut, though, and the judge calmly told him to proceed, even as Stewart thundered: "I except to it with all the vehemence of my nature!" The petition was signed by four churchmen. If prayer was to open each session of the court, they would like to see a little variety in the praying, they felt. There are many people involved in the trial, they argued, "to whom the prayers of the fundamentalists are not spiritually uplifting and are occasionally offensive."

Judge Raulston's response brought a great burst of laughter: "I shall refer that petition to the pastors' association of this town." Since the association was made up largely of fundamentalist ministers, the newsmen thought at first that the judge was cracking a joke. But he was quite serious. And the laughter, in fact, was soon drowned by applause.

Judge Raulston was serious, too, when he turned to the next matter. He began by explaining how impossible it would be for anyone to learn of his decision on quashing in an honest manner. Then he said: "I am informed that the newspapers in the large cities are being now sold which undertake to state what my opinion is." He announced that court would adjourn until the next morning, but he wanted to meet with the newsmen about this matter now.

After the courtroom was cleared of spectators, Judge Raulston read the newsmen a telegram: ST LOUIS STAR OUT FINAL CARRYING STORY LAW BEEN HELD CONSTITUTIONAL BY JUDGE.

The judge then appointed a committee of five newsmen to investigate the story and its origin. William Hutchinson was not one of the five.

CHAPTER NINE
WITNESS

Well!"

The Wednesday session had been under way for a short while when Judge Raulston uttered that solitary word. The judge was seldom at a loss for words. But he had just been informed that it was Judge Raulston himself who had leaked the decision on quashing. While Raulston sat speechless, the spokesman for the newsman investigators he had appointed explained how Hutchinson had come up with the forbidden information by "pure deduction." Raulston recovered enough to give Hutchinson a short lecture on fair and unfair questions. But in the end he had to forgive him.

Wednesday morning was destined to be a time for forgiveness. Attorney General Stewart had already apologized to Hays for telling him on Tuesday to keep his mouth shut. And Hays had happily forgiven him his rash remarks.

Stewart's apology to Hays, though, had led Neal to suggest that the attorney general should make another one: "I ask him in public to erase from the record the slurring, discourteous remark that he made in regard to another colleague of mine in this case," said Neal. "And he knows very well what I refer to!"

What Neal referred to was Stewart's calling Darrow an agnostic. But Stewart was in no mood for a second apology. "So long as I speak what I conceive to be the truth, I apologize to no man!"

When he got a chance, Darrow rose to answer Stewart. "I don't want the court to think I take any exception to

Mr. Stewart's statement," he began. "Of course, the weather is warm," he said with a smile, "and we may all go a little further at times than we ought. But he is perfectly justified in saying that I am an agnostic, for I am. And I do not consider it an insult but rather a compliment to be called an agnostic." Then he explained what Stewart was really accusing him of. "I do not pretend to know," he said, "where many ignorant men are sure." Added Darrow, with an expressive shrug of his shoulders: "That is all agnosticism means."

After Darrow had said his piece, Judge Raulston finally got around to what was now an anticlimax—and a dull one at that—the reading of his opinion on the motion to quash. But first the event had to be recorded on film. As he called for order so that he might be heard, he turned to the photographers. "If you gentlemen want to take my picture," he said, "take it now." To the crowd, Raulston's love for being photographed had become a joke. They broke out laughing.

Five minutes later, after the photographers had enough pictures of the judge grasping the opinion in his left hand, Raulston began his reading. What he had to say about the thirteen grounds that Neal had given for quashing couldn't be much of a surprise now. But it probably wouldn't have been anyway. His comments about the Butler Act could easily have been written by the prosecution. "It gives no preference to any particular religion," he had decided. And it doesn't restrict freedom of speech: "There is no law in the State of Tennessee that undertakes to compel this defendant, or any other citizen, to accept employment in the public schools." He ended by stating that he was "now pleased to overrule the whole motion and require the defendant to plead further." The trial, in other words, must go on.

And so on Wednesday afternoon the twelve men who had been so pleased on the past Friday to be named jurors for the great show to come, were called into court. The time had at last arrived for them to hear the evidence in the case of the State of Tennessee versus John Thomas Scopes.

Once the jury discovered what they were missing, though, they may have wished they were back outside on the courthouse lawn where a breeze might now and then stir the hot air. "If it ain't out of order," said the foreman of the jury, "I would like to make the request—the unanimous request of the jury—to take up the matter of some electric fans here. This heat is fearful!" The judge offered to share his small fan, then promised to look into the matter.

As the trial of John Scopes at last went forward, it sounded as if it would be quickly finished. "What is your plea, gentlemen?" asked Raulston. "Not guilty, may it please your honor," answered Neal. Then Stewart delivered the shortest opening statement for the prosecution that could be imagined: "It is the insistence of the State in this case that the defendant, John Thomas Scopes, has violated the antievolution law—what is known as the an-

tievolution law—by teaching in the public schools of Rhea County the theory tending to show that man and mankind is descended from a lower order of animals." Concluded Stewart: "Therefore, he has taught a theory which denies the story of divine creation of man as taught by the Bible."

And why should the defense disagree with the State? Why not quickly admit Scopes's guilt and get the trial over with? Then the verdict could be appealed to a higher court where the issue of constitutionality could certainly be argued again.

But as Dudley Field Malone began the opening statement for the defense, it soon became evident that the case would not end so simply. "We will prove," said Malone, "that whether this statute be constitutional or unconstitutional, the defendant Scopes did not and could not violate it."

As Malone talked on, the line that the defense would take became clear. It was not enough to show that John Scopes had taught about evolution. It was also necessary to show that teaching about evolution denies the biblical story of creation. The defense will prove, said Malone, "that there is more than one theory of creation set forth in the Bible, and that they are conflicting." They will also show, he went on, "that there are millions of people who believe in evolution and in the stories of creation as set forth in the Bible and who find no conflict between the two."

Malone made it clear that the defense would make good use of experts—not only experts on the Bible and its meaning, but experts on science. "We shall prove by experts and scientists in every field of scientific knowledge that there is no branch of science which can be taught today without teaching the theory of evolution."

For most of the audience, the big event of Malone's presentation came from Bryan. Malone dragged Bryan's name into his discussion repeatedly. "There may be a conflict between evolution and the peculiar ideas of Christianity which are held by Mr. Bryan," he said at one point. Then, pressing the idea that Bryan's brand of Christianity wasn't the only one, he suggested: "The defense maintains that there is a clear distinction between God, the Church, the Bible, Christianity, and Mr. Bryan." Finally Malone quoted from Bryan's earlier writings to show that he once argued for a free search for truth. That didn't sound like the Bryan of today.

Malone was obviously trying to needle Bryan. But the only one who seemed disturbed by his attack on Bryan was the attorney general. Stewart finally objected to the way Malone was hurling Bryan's name about. Judge Raulston agreed with him and sustained the objection.

Bryan, though, was unconcerned—at least he tried to give that impression. His face was red as he got to his feet to comment, but reporters blamed that on the heat. "I ask no protection from the court," he said. "When the proper time comes," he added in a menacing tone that delighted his fans, "I shall be able to show the gentleman that I stand today just where I did, but that this has nothing to do with the case at bar." The audience, obviously thirsting for words from their idol, applauded his little speech vigorously.

The opening remarks ended with a laugh, courtesy of General McKenzie. "The only mistake the good Lord made," he said to Malone, "is that he did not withhold the completion of the job until he could have got a conference with you." Replied Malone: "I rather think you are right." When the laughter died, the jury was finally sworn in and the testimony in the case against John Scopes began.

First on the witness stand was the superintendent of schools. He testified that Scopes had indeed taught in the Rhea County Central High School and had used Hunter's *Civic Biology* in his teaching. According to the superintendent, Scopes had also admitted that he couldn't teach from that book without teaching evolution.

The superintendent was followed by one of Scopes's students, Howard Morgan, who agreed that "Professor Scopes" had taught him about evolution. "There was a little germ of one cell organism formed," he said, as he explained what Scopes had taught, "and this organism kept evolving until it got to be a pretty good-sized animal, and then it came on to be a land animal, and it kept on evolving, and from this was man."

Later in the questioning, Stewart probed further: "How did he classify man with reference to other animals? What did he say about them?"

"Well, the book and he both classified man along with cats and dogs, cows, horses, monkeys, lions, horses, and all that," said Howard.

"What did he say they were?"

"Mammals," said Howard.

When it was Darrow's turn to cross-examine Howard, he carried the questioning further. "Now, Howard, what do you mean by classify?"

Howard stumbled: "Well, it means classify these animals we mentioned—that men were just the same as them. In other words . . ."

"He didn't say a cat was the same as a man?" asked Darrow.

"No, sir," answered Howard. "He said man had a reasoning power, that these animals did not."

"There is some doubt about that!" said Darrow. The audience laughed heartily as the judge called for order.

Darrow tried to find what Howard knew about mammals but found he didn't really know much of anything. Failing there, Darrow asked: "Well, did he tell you anything else that was wicked?"

"No," said Howard. "Not that I remember of."

After Darrow reviewed more of what Scopes had taught Howard, he stopped and asked abruptly: "It has not hurt you any, has it?"

"No, sir," said Howard, as the audience laughed.

There was more to the case for the prosecution, but it was mostly the same story repeated. Everybody agreed that John Scopes had taught about evolution in Rhea County Central High School. And of course the defense agreed too. But did that mean that Scopes had broken the law? The defense hoped to prove that it didn't.

The afternoon was already well along when the defense opened its case. There was some question whether they had a case, for the prosecution had already made it known that they would object to any expert testimony. And that was what the whole case for the defense rested on. Eight scientists had come to Dayton to explain evolution. And four biblical scholars had also come to town to explain the Bible. After these explanations, hoped the defense, everybody would agree that Scopes did not break the law after all.

First on the stand was Maynard M. Metcalf, a professor of zoology from Johns Hopkins University. "A somewhat chubby man of bland mien," Mencken labeled him. Darrow had just started to question Metcalf when Stewart interrupted. Of course Darrow expected the attorney general to object to the scientific testimony that was about to come. But Metcalf hadn't even admitted he was a scientist yet. It turned out that Stewart wanted to point out that Tennessee has a rule that the defendant has to take the stand first or not at all. If John Scopes was to speak in his own defense, he had to speak at the outset.

"Well," said Darrow, "you've already caught me on it."

"That is a technicality . . ." said Judge Raulston, "I will allow you to withdraw the witness."

But Darrow had no interest in his offer. "Your honor, every single word that was said against this defendant—everything—was true."

"So he does not care to go on the stand?"

"No," answered Darrow. "What is the use?"

And so John Scopes, on trial for breaking the law, would have no part in pleading his case. "So I sat speechless," he later remarked, "a ringside observer at my own trial, until the end of the circus."

Darrow's main reason for keeping him from the stand, Scopes decided, was to avoid revealing that he wasn't really a dedicated biology teacher. "Darrow realized that I was not a science teacher," said Scopes, "and he was afraid that if I were put on the stand I would be asked if I actually taught biology."

Zoologist Metcalf was there to give a lesson on evolution, of course. And in the end he gave rather a good one —but not to the jury. As soon as Darrow began directing his remarks to evolution, Stewart began objecting.

"Are you an evolutionist?" Darrow had asked.

"Surely," answered Metcalf quickly. Then he added with a smile: "Under certain circumstances that question would be an insult. Under these circumstances I do not regard it as such."

"Do you know any scientific man in the world that is not an evolutionist?" continued Darrow. But that was Stewart's cue: "We except to that, of course."

The battle of "admissibility" had begun. Just who believed in evolution had nothing to do with the case, in Stewart's mind. The jury shouldn't hear any of that sort of talk. And they shouldn't be around while the attorneys argue about whether they should hear it, either.

After some discussion the jury was excused once again, this time with a warning not to listen to the speakers that blared outside the courthouse. The jury foreman appeared hurt. "I just wanted to say for the benefit of the jury," he said, "there is not a single juryman that has heard a single word pass over the horns out there."

With the jury gone, Metcalf's scientific testimony was permitted to go on. Judge Raulston, it certainly appeared, was interested himself in hearing more about evolution. And if he was going to rule on the admissibility of expert testimony, he needed to know just what sort of testimony he was ruling on.

"Evolution and the theories of evolution," began Metcalf, "are fundamentally different things." Scientists are in full agreement that evolution had occurred, but not about how. "The fact of evolution is a thing that is perfectly and absolutely clear," he argued. "But there are dozens of theories of evolution, some of which are almost wholly absurd, some of which are surely largely mistaken, some of which are perhaps almost wholly true."

Metcalf discussed how much was then known—and how little—about the origins of life. Darrow quizzed him about how long ago life began on earth. Metcalf hesitated to answer. The matter of years wasn't really in his field. "I would have to be answering what I have heard from others, and I don't like to testify to that kind of stuff."

But Darrow persisted: "More than six thousand years ago, wasn't it?" He was referring to the fundamentalist idea that man was created at about that time. The idea had started with James Ussher, an Irish archbishop, who had made a close study of the words of the Bible in the middle of the 17th century and decided from them that man was created in 4004 B.C.

"Well," said Metcalf, "six hundred million years ago is a very modest guess." In 1925 Metcalf didn't realize just how modest he was being—at least from a scientist's point of view. Since then, the remains of life have been found imbedded in rocks that are measured to be several billion years old.

It had been a long day, everyone agreed, as Darrow asked his last question. "And you say that evolution as you speak of it means including man?"

Metcalf's answer was mercifully short: "Surely." The court adjourned until Thursday at nine.

CHAPTER TEN
EACH A
MIGHTY VOICE

For most of the audience, the Thursday morning session was dull. The bickering about the correct procedure for arguing about expert testimony seemed endless—and pointless. Should Metcalf finish his testimony now or later? Should the defense or the prosecution give the opening and closing arguments?

When all the little legal details were worked out, the arguments on admissibility began. And to start with, at least, that wasn't much more exciting. Bryan's son led off for the prosecution, and it soon became evident that he had not inherited his father's genius for oratory. Hays then gave the arguments for the defense. Sue Hicks and General Ben McKenzie followed him, trying to tear apart any arguments Hays had managed to stick together. There was a lot of talk, but nothing much new in the way of ideas. Of course with General McKenzie holding forth, there was sure to be something new in the way of humor.

"They want to put words into God's mouth," complained McKenzie about the defense, "and have him say that he issued some sort of protoplasm or soft dishrag and put it in the ocean and said: 'Old boy, if you wait around about six thousand years, I will make something of you.' " Of course McKenzie was twisting the words of his opponents. The defense hadn't tried to suggest how life began —whether by God-created "dishrag" or other means. And they had certainly suggested that any "dishrag" would have taken considerably more than six thousand years to evolve into man. But the general's remark was good for a moment of welcome laughter.

If Thursday morning was not a memorable session in the Scopes trial, the same would never be said about Thursday afternoon. The word had gotten around that the Great Commoner would end his courtroom silence by arguing against the admission of expert testimony. "Word that the great Bryan was going to speak made the courthouse a magnet," wrote one reporter, "and long before the time set for the afternoon session, the crowds filled the courtroom, sweltered in the halls and stairways, begged entrance, and took every inch of space within the lawyers' arena and on the judge's rostrum."

"There was hardly room for the lawyers to maneuver," continued the reporter, "but it was not much of a law case anyway and no one minded. Here they realized was one of the greatest shows in the world."

The Thursday afternoon session began with a warning from Judge Raulston not to get too excited because of the great weight on the floor. "I do not know how well it is supported, but sometimes buildings and floors give way when they are unduly burdened," he warned. "So I suggest to you to be as quiet in the courtroom as you can. Have no more emotion than you can avoid. Especially have no applause, because it isn't proper in the courtroom."

But with the great Bryan rising to speak, the audience could be counted on to ignore the judge's words. This was a moment they had waited almost a week to see. Their hero had at last agreed to enter the battle, and the faithful would surely cheer him on.

The Commoner appeared to have dressed up for his speech. He hadn't gone so far as to wear a coat. It was still too hot for such formality—except for such unbelievable "dudes" as Dudley Field Malone. But his pale purple shirt bore a soft collar, and he wore a black bow tie around his throat.

"If the court please," began Bryan, "we are now approaching the end of the first week of this trial, and I haven't thought it proper until this time to take part in the discussions."

The prosecution's argument against expert testimony was simple, and when he got through his many opening remarks Bryan repeated it anew: "This is not the place to try to prove that the law ought never to have been passed. The place to prove that, or teach that, was to the legislature." The experts were obviously here just to show what a great idea evolution is—an idea that the people of Tennessee should never make laws against. "Your honor, it isn't proper to bring experts in here to try to defeat the purpose of the people of this state," said Bryan, "by trying to show that this thing that they denounce and outlaw is a beautiful thing that everybody ought to believe in."

Bryan drew a laugh with an example of the sort of thing he claimed the defense was trying to do: "If a man made a contract with somebody to bring rain in a dry season down here, and if he was to have $500 for an inch of rain, and if the rain did not come and he sued to enforce his contract and collect the money, could he bring experts in to prove that a drought was better than a rain?"

But if Bryan was sure that it wasn't proper for experts to talk about what a beautiful thing evolution is, he didn't hesitate himself to talk about what an ugly thing it is.

"On page 194 we have a diagram," said Bryan, holding up a copy of Hunter's *Civic Biology,* "and this diagram purports to give someone's family tree." The diagram included circles for various different groups of animals. To Bryan the diagram was an object of fun. Referring to the numbers of species, which were shown for each group, he cracked: "I see they are round numbers, and I don't think all of these animals breed in round numbers." The sponges, with the help of a pun, gave him another chance for a laugh: "Thirty-five hundred sponges? I am satisfied from some I have seen there must be more than thirty-five thousand sponges!"

But Bryan saved his biggest jests for the circle that held the mammals: "And then we have the mammals—thirty-five hundred. And there is a little circle, and man is in the circle. Find him! Find man!"

"There is the book," exclaimed Bryan, his voice filling the room—"there is the book where they were teaching your children that man was a mammal, and so indistinguishable among mammals that they leave him there with thirty-four hundred and ninety-nine other mammals— including elephants! Talk about putting Daniel in the lion's den! How dared those scientists put man in a little ring like that with lions and tigers and everything that is bad!''

Bryan, it appeared, was no lover of animals—nonhuman animals, at any rate. He went on to complain how the scientists could possibly think of "shutting man up in a little circle like that with all these animals that have an odor that extends beyond the circumference of this circle, my friends." The audience, themselves shut up on a hot July day with plainly odorous members of their own species, were still able to laugh long and loud at Bryan's jesting.

At one point Bryan got a laugh by quoting from Darwin's second book on evolution, *The Descent of Man*. In that book Darwin spoke of the evolution of the apes and monkeys—called the Simiadae at that time. "The Simiadae then branched off into two great stems," quoted Bryan, "the New World and the Old World monkeys. And from the latter, at a remote period, man, the wonder and glory of the universe, proceeded." Spreading his arms before the audience, Bryan complained: "Not even from American monkeys, but from Old World monkeys!" The crowd roared.

"Now here we have our glorious pedigree," he scoffed as he continued. "And each child is expected to copy the family tree and take it home to his family to be substituted for the Bible family tree. That is what Darwin says!"

Plainly addressing the audience, Bryan continued: "Now my friends . . ." But he stopped and apologized to Judge Raulston: "I beg your pardon, if the court please.

I have been so in the habit of talking to an audience instead of a court that I will sometimes say 'my friends' . . ." Then he added an afterthought: ". . . although I happen to know not all of them are my friends!" The audience laughed. It was a good show.

"The facts are simple," said Bryan as he neared the end of his speech. "The case is plain. And if those gentlemen want to enter upon a larger field of educational work on the subject of evolution, let them get through with this case and then convene a mock court." As forbidden applause echoed through the fragile courtroom, he brought his address to a close: "For it would deserve the title of mock court if its purpose is to banish from the hearts of the people the word of God as revealed!"

The judge sat silent and made no move to stop the applause. It was the big event of the day—in fact, the big event of the trial, perhaps. The idol of Dayton had spewed forth his best curses upon evolution, and the walls would surely not tumble as he was cheered for his godly act.

If those words had closed the session, Thursday would have been remembered as Bryan's day. But the cheers of Dayton were to find that day a new and unexpected object. And the people of Dayton on that Thursday evening would tell each other that Bryan was losing his touch. He wasn't the same Bryan who had talked of a cross of gold.

As Dudley Field Malone rose later to answer Bryan's arguments, he still wore the jacket that for many steaming Dayton days had set him apart from most of the other occupants of the stifling courtroom. But then he performed "the most effective act anyone could have thought of to get the audience's undivided attention," as Scopes later described it. He carefully took his jacket off, folded it neatly, and laid it on the defense counsels' table.

As he began, all eyes were upon him: "If the court please, it does seem to me that we have gone far afield in this discussion." But he soon made it clear that he might go rather far afield himself.

"Whether Mr. Bryan knows it or not, he is a mammal, he is an animal, and he is a man." There was a hint of weariness in his voice.

"He was not liked," wrote one reporter about Malone. "When he began the people were against him. They do not like New York where he comes from. They do not like his clothes nor his accent." But then the reporter added: "But he had not been speaking more than ten minutes before there was a change."

Warming to his subject, Malone complained of the limits the fundamentalists would put on knowledge. "Are we to have our children know nothing about science except what the church says they shall know?" he asked at one point. "I have never seen harm in learning and understanding, in humility and open-mindedness." Then he aimed a sharp insult at the prosecution: "And I have never seen clearer the need of that learning than when I see the attitude of the prosecution, who attack and refuse to accept the information and intelligence which expert witnesses will give them."

Malone's speech began quietly. But it built rapidly to a roar. "It roared out of the open windows like the sound of artillery practice, and alarmed the moonshiners and catamounts on distant peaks," wrote H. L. Mencken, taking some liberties in his description. "Trains thundering by on the nearby railroad sounded faint and far away." Then giving in completely to his flight of fancy, Mencken added: "The yokels outside stuffed their Bibles into the loudspeaker horns and yielded themselves joyously to the impact of the original. In brief, Malone was in good voice."

Much of Malone's speech was a plea for Bryan to come out and fight—to wage that "duel to the death" he had promised. "My old chief," pled Malone, recalling the days when he worked for Bryan in the State Department: "I never saw him back away from a great issue before. I feel that the prosecution here is filled with a needless fear. I believe that if they withdraw their objection and hear the evidence of our experts, their minds would not only be improved, but their souls would be purified."

Malone frequently accused the prosecution of being afraid of knowledge. Speaking again for the children, he urged: "The least that this generation can do, your honor, is to give the next generation all the facts, all the available data, all the theories, all the information that learning, that study, that observation has produced. Give it to the children in the hope of heaven that they will make a better world of this than we have been able to make it."

Then, referring to World War I that was still fresh in memory, he went on: "We have just had a war with twenty

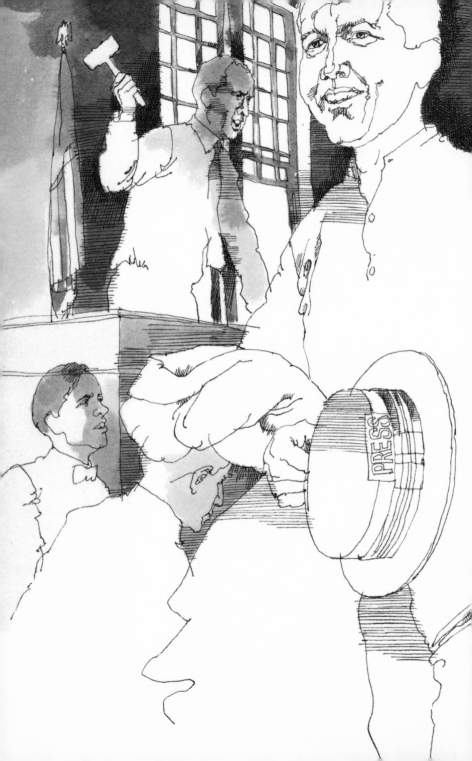

"Dudley," said H. L. Mencken as he shook Malone's hand,
"That was the loudest speech I ever heard."

million dead. Civilization is not so proud of the work of adults. Civilization need not be so proud of what the grownups have done. For God's sake let the children have their minds kept open. Close no doors to their knowledge. Shut no door for them!"

Malone's speech was loud but not long. It soon thundered to a close. "We are not afraid," he boomed. "Where is the fear? We meet it! Where is the fear? We defy it! We ask your honor to admit the evidence as a matter of correct law, as a matter of sound procedure, and as a matter of justice to the defense in this case."

The speech ended in a riot of applause that the judge tried vainly to stop. "At its end they gave it a tremendous cheer," reported Mencken—"a cheer at least four times as hearty as that given to Bryan. For these rustics delight in speechifying, and know when it is good."

A policeman pounded so hard on a table that it split. When another policeman came to help him restore order, he shouted: "I'm not trying to get order. I'm cheering!"

Many rushed forward to congratulate Malone. Even Mencken struggled through the crowd to clasp his hand. "Dudley," he said, "that was the loudest speech I ever heard."

The afternoon session wasn't over, but little notice was made of what followed. The society lawyer from New York City had taken the day.

When the court had adjourned and the crowd had wandered off, three men were slow to leave. William Jennings Bryan sat quite alone in his rocking chair by the prosecution's table, staring straight ahead. Fanning himself with his palm-leaf fan seemed almost too much an effort, but occasionally he would stir the warm air of the courtroom toward his face. At the defense counsel's table sat John Scopes and Dudley Field Malone.

Still staring straight ahead, Bryan said in a quiet voice: "Dudley, that was the greatest speech I have ever heard."

"Thank you, Mr. Bryan," said Malone. And then he added, as if he had turned against his own father: "I am sorry it was I who had to make it."

CHAPTER ELEVEN
NO TIME
FOR LEARNING

L ike the day, Thursday night was also stormy in Dayton. But it was not man that created this storm. Lightning streaked across the sky and thunder echoed through the Tennessee hills.

Darrow was at the Mansion discussing the case with the other defense lawyers and the experts whose fate in court was probably being decided at that moment. The Mansion was a large, deserted house—some Daytonians said it was haunted—that George Rappleyea had fixed up for any of the defense who needed housing. Although Darrow and his wife had been put up in a private house, most of the rest stayed at the Mansion.

The faded wooden structure stood on a small hill about a mile from Dayton, exposed to the full fury of the summer storm. As the time between flash and sound grew shorter, Darrow raised his eyes skyward and said with a smile: "Boys, if lightning strikes this house tonight . . ."

The storm washed the dusty streets of Dayton and gave a few moments of relief from the heat. Dayton awoke to "a fresh wind blowing from the hills," wrote a newsman. But the relief was destined to be all too short.

As the spectators walked toward the courthouse to see what drama Friday might offer, the memory of the day before was still fresh. "They were still talking of their disappointment in Bryan," observed one reporter, "the spectacle of this old gladiator of many battles tumbled in the dust by the shining spear of Dudley Field Malone's logic."

After the opening prayer, Judge Raulston read his decision on the experts. It hadn't been leaked, but it was hardly a surprise. The defense may have won the battle of speeches, but that battle had no effect on the decision. It was a good show, but it didn't quite make it as an argument—at least not with the judge.

"In the final analysis . . ." said Raulston, as he approached the end of his reading, "after a most earnest and careful consideration . . ." But his earnest and careful consideration hadn't changed what had seemed to be his feelings. The only question, the judge had concluded after his deep thought, was whether John Scopes had taught "the theory that man descended from a lower order of animals." By the wording of the Butler Act, that was the same thing as denying the divine story of creation. And it wouldn't really matter if every scientist in the world was convinced that man did descend from a lower order of animals. And it wouldn't really matter either if every biblical scholar in the world was convinced that a lowly descent did not deny the divine story of creation. The only question was still: Did John Thomas Scopes teach the theory that man descended from a lower order of animals?

"If the court is correct in this," said Judge Raulston, "then the evidence of experts would shed no light on the issues. Therefore, the court is content to sustain the motion of the attorney general to exclude the expert testimony."

The defense lawyers were hardly taken by surprise by the judge's decision. Yet they obviously were bitter. Their last hope of making a case had been taken from them. They had freely admitted that John Scopes had taught that man had descended from a lower order of animals. If that was to be the only issue, they had lost the case already.

Hays rose to complain about the verdict. And his remarks were so harsh that Tom Stewart felt he should defend the court. "I think it is a reflection upon the court," he protested.

"Well," drawled Raulston, with more good nature than Stewart could show, "it don't hurt this court."

"I think there is no danger of it hurting the court, for that matter," agreed Stewart.

"There is no danger of it hurting us," said Darrow.

"No," said Stewart, "you are already hurt as much as you can be hurt."

"Don't worry about us," shot back Darrow. "The State of Tennessee don't rule the world yet!"

The mission of the defense was now to get as much into the record as they could. The case at hand was a lost cause, but not the appeal that was sure to come. When the case went to a higher court, that court should have all the evidence before it—including the expert testimony that Judge Raulston wouldn't permit now.

Fortunately Judge Raulston agreed. The defense could read into the record the testimony that would have been given by the scientists and by the Bible experts. Of course the jury couldn't hear any of it. It had been overruled for their ears. But everybody else could hear it.

With many tempers short, even working out that agreement did not go smoothly. Speaking of the experts' statements, Darrow asked: "Can we have the rest of the day to draft them?"

"I would not say . . ." began Judge Raulston, in what Darrow took to be a protest.

"If your honor takes a half day to write an opinion . . ." said Darrow, obviously referring to the delay in getting the court's opinion on the motion to quash the indictment.

Raulston objected: "I have not taken . . ."

But Darrow butted in again: "We want to make statements here of what we expect to prove. I do not understand why every request of the State and every suggestion of the prosecution should meet with an endless waste of time, and a bare suggestion of anything that is perfectly competent on our part should be immediately overruled." The counsel for the defense was clearly irked.

"I hope," said Raulston, "you do not mean to reflect upon the court."

"Well," came back Darrow, speaking in measured tones, "your honor has the right to hope!"

As Darrow stood with his shoulders hunched forward, his expressive face underlining his words, the audience laughed. But not Raulston. Feeling Darrow was perilously close to contempt of court, he frowned and added: "I have the right to do something else, perhaps."

"All right," said Darrow, as he turned away, now smiling. "All right."

A short while later Raulston went along with Darrow's suggestion and adjourned the court for the day—in fact, the week. It was Friday and the court would not meet again till Monday morning at nine.

The judge's decision to exclude expert testimony wasn't applauded by all the locals. The food and drink vendors, fundamentalist or not, didn't want to see the trial end so quickly. Business hadn't been as brisk as they had hoped, and they needed more time to make up for the money they had spent on building stands and renting space.

And another fundamentalist, surprisingly, also wasn't pleased. As John Washington Butler chatted with other reporters after adjournment, he expressed his regret: "I'd like to have heard the evidence. It would have been right smart of an education to hear those fellows who have studied the subject." But he hadn't changed his mind about the Butler Act, he said. He still felt it was a good law and he was happy to have written it. Apparently children should be spared the education he wanted to hear.

Many newsmen decided the trial was over—or at least close enough to it. There would be the expert testimony to be read into the record and a few other formalities to go through. Then the case would go to the jury, who would quickly decide Scopes was guilty as charged. The judge would then fine Scopes as the law required, and the ACLU would pay the fine and make arrangements to have the case appealed. It looked routine.

One of the newsmen who left town was H. L. Mencken. Some people said, though, that he left for another reason. Those mountaineers with squirrel guns had been hearing what Mencken was writing about the locals and weren't taking too kindly to it. At least that was the story.

Almost as if they were part of an act, Bryan and Darrow both kept the case alive over the weekend. Darrow, frustrated at every turn, still sounded like a man who wanted to fight the good fight. "Bryan, who blew the loud trumpet calling for a 'battle to the death,' has fled from the field, his forces disorganized," he commented. Could Darrow really imagine that the elusive Bryan might still agree to do battle?

John Scopes spent a lazy weekend. On Sunday morning he went to church—"as usual." In the afternoon he went for a swim in the pool where he had taken the newsmen. Dayton's temperature was reaching new heights.

CHAPTER TWELVE
THE LAWN PARTY

The first official act of Judge John T. Raulston on Monday, the 20th of July, was to cite Clarence Darrow for contempt of court. "The court has withheld any action until passion had time to subdue," began the citation. In fact, it seemed that it might have been the other way around. After Judge Raulston had thought over what Darrow had said to him on Friday, he got mad about it. Or perhaps Tom Stewart convinced him he should be mad about it. "He who would hurl contempt into the records of my court," read the citation, "insults and outrages the good people of one of the greatest states of the Union." There was no way out, Raulston decided, but to cite the high and mighty lawyer who had sneered at this Tennessee court.

The rest of the morning was routine. Hays read endlessly as statements by experts on evolution and on the Bible became a part of the record. The words he read were often interesting and always educational. But it wasn't the same as testimony with its give and take between the witness and the examiner or the cross-examiner.

The statement of one expert quoted a letter that Bryan's former boss, Woodrow Wilson, had written during the summer of 1922. President Wilson had been accused of rejecting the notion of evolution. In answer to that charge he wrote: "May it not suffice for me to say, in reply to your letter of August 25th, that, of course, like every other man of intelligence and education, I do believe in organic evolution. It surprises me that at this late date such questions should be raised."

The statements were interesting, but hardly exciting. The day, though, was not through with excitement.

The afternoon session began with the same subject as the morning session—contempt of court. But Clarence Darrow, rather than Judge Raulston, had the floor: "I have been practicing law for 47 years, and I have been pretty busy. And most of the time in court I have had many a case where I have had to do what I have been doing here—fighting the public opinion of the people in the community where I was trying the case—even in my own town. And I never yet have, in all my time, had any criticism by the court for anything I have done in court."

Darrow wasn't quite ready to admit that his remark was actually contempt of court, but he was willing to apologize for it: "Personally I don't think it constitutes a contempt, but I am quite certain that the remark should not have been made, and the court could not help taking notice of it, and I am sorry that I made it ever since I got time to read it, and I want to apologize to the court for it."

Judge Raulston beamed as the audience applauded. That was what he needed to restore the "dignity" of the court. He would be happy to forgive Darrow—not, though, without benefit of a short sermon: "My friends and Colonel Darrow, the man that I believe came into the world to save man from sin, the man that died on the cross that man might be redeemed, taught that it was godly to forgive." After a final quotation from the Bible, Judge Raulston and Clarence Darrow shook hands and the incident was over.

Judge Raulston then made an unusual proposal: "I think the court should adjourn downstairs. I am afraid of the building. The court will convene down in the yard." There had been a rumor that cracks had appeared in the ceiling below. "It made a good story," remarked Scopes years later. But Scopes had a different theory: "Even the judge, who had an electric fan that the rest of us didn't share, couldn't stand the man-killing heat, which had not let up."

A platform had been erected in the shade of the oaks and maples on the courthouse lawn. Earlier it had been the scene of Bryan's Sunday sermonizing, and it still bore some of the marks. A huge banner advising READ YOUR BIBLE hung on the courthouse wall nearby. Now the platform became the scene for the dying moments of the Monkey Trial.

It was a strange "courtroom" as Hays continued reading experts' statements into the record. The judge's desk was located on the platform, along with the witness stand, but the defense and prosecution tables were on the ground. There were a few benches, but most of the audience stood or sat here and there about the lawn. A few sat on the hoods of cars parked nearby or stood on the running boards to get a better view.

When Hays had finished his reading, Darrow suggested that something should be done about that banner: "I move that it be removed."

It seemed an obvious request, but General McKenzie wasn't going to let it go easily: "If your honor please, why should it be removed? It is their defense, and stated before the court, that they do not deny the Bible." Others of the prosecution joined in, including Bryan. It was too good a chance to pass up.

But Darrow was up to the challenge. "We might agree to get up a sign of equal size on the other side and in the same position," he offered, "reading HUNTER'S BIOLOGY or READ YOUR EVOLUTION." In the end Judge Raulston ordered the banner taken down.

Hays, the man in charge of technicalities, then offered a Catholic Bible and a Hebrew Bible as evidence—evidence that would obviously be no use now but might serve in the appeal. The appeal court might agree that "the Bible" mentioned in the Butler Act could mean quite different things to different people.

And then the big event of the day began to unfold. Hays told the judge that the defense would like to call another witness. Malone, who was sitting next to Scopes, turned to whisper: "Hell is going to pop now!"

"The defense desires to call Mr. Bryan as a witness," said Hays. Then he explained: "We should like to take Mr. Bryan's testimony for the purposes of our record." The defense wanted to present Bryan as an expert witness—an expert on the Bible.

The prosecution lawyers—except Bryan—leapt to their feet to protest. Judge Raulston was obviously taken by surprise: "Do you think you have a right . . ." he began weakly.

The request was obviously irregular and Bryan could easily have refused to take the stand. But it soon became clear that Bryan would welcome the chance to talk again —especially if he could do some questioning himself afterwards.

"If your honor please, I insist that Mr. Darrow can be put on the stand," said Bryan, "and Mr. Malone and Mr. Hays."

"Call anybody you desire. Ask them any questions you wish," said Raulston.

"Then," said Bryan, "we will call all three of them."

"Not at once?" joked Darrow.

Unamused, Bryan asked the judge: "Where do you want me to sit?"

By now Raulston had recovered from Hays's surprise move and was beginning to wonder whether this was the thing to do. "Mr. Bryan," he said earnestly, "you are not objecting to going on the stand?"

"Not at all!" said Bryan, as he mounted the platform and took his seat.

"You have given considerable study to the Bible, haven't you, Mr. Bryan?" began Darrow.

"Yes, sir. I have tried to."

The examination began slowly. Since Bryan was testifying as an expert on the Bible, his qualifications had to be established.

"I have studied the Bible for about fifty years, or some time more than that," said the 65-year-old Bryan. "But of course, I've studied it more as I have become older than when I was but a boy."

"Do you claim that everything in the Bible should be literally interpreted?" asked Darrow.

"I believe everything in the Bible should be accepted as it is given there."

Darrow turned first to the story of Jonah. After quizzing Bryan on what kind of fish it was that swallowed Jonah, Darrow said: "Now you say the big fish swallowed Jonah, and he there remained—how long?—three days, and then he spewed him upon the land. You believe that the big fish was made to swallow Jonah?"

"I am not prepared to say that," answered Bryan. "The Bible merely says it was done."

"You don't know whether it was the ordinary run of fish," pursued Darrow, "or made for that purpose?"

"You may guess," shot back Bryan. "You evolutionists guess."

"But when we guess," said Darrow, "we have a sense to guess right."

"But do not do it often," challenged Bryan.

"You are not prepared to say whether that fish was made especially to swallow a man or not?" continued Darrow.

"The Bible doesn't say," said Bryan. "So I am not prepared to say."

"You don't know whether that was fixed up specially for the purpose?"

"No," repeated Bryan. "The Bible doesn't say."

"But do you believe he made them—that he made such

a fish," said Darrow, "and that it was big enough to swallow Jonah?"

"Yes, sir," said Bryan. "Let me add: One miracle is just as easy to believe as another."

"It is for me!" agreed Darrow.

"It is for me!" came back Bryan, forcing a different meaning into the words.

Darrow went from Jonah to Joshua: "Do you believe Joshua made the sun stand still?"

"I believe what the Bible says," said Bryan. "I suppose you mean that the earth stood still?"

"I don't know. I am talking about the Bible now."

"I accept the Bible absolutely," said Bryan.

Darrow went on: "The Bible says Joshua commanded the sun to stand still for the purpose of lengthening the day, doesn't it? And you believe it?"

"I do," said Bryan.

"Do you believe at that time the entire sun went around the earth?" asked Darrow.

"No," said Bryan. "I believe that the earth goes around the sun."

"Do you believe that the men who wrote it thought that the day could be lengthened if the sun could be stopped?"

"I don't know what they thought," said Bryan.

"You don't know?" said Darrow.

"I think they wrote the fact without expressing their own thoughts," said Bryan.

"Have you any opinion as to whether or not the men who wrote that thought . . ."

At that point Attorney General Stewart butted in to object to the whole line of questioning. But it was obvious that Raulston was enjoying the examination. And Bryan himself had no thought of calling it quits, though he was clearly losing his earlier confidence as Darrow's probing continued.

Darrow tried to get Bryan to admit that the story of Joshua had to be interpreted in the light of science as it was understood at that time. But Bryan wasn't ready to admit that the Bible ever needed to be interpreted.

After he had disposed of Joshua, Darrow quizzed Bryan on the date of man's creation. Bishop Ussher, whose estimates were printed in the edition of the Bible that had been presented as evidence, had set creation at 4004 B.C. "That estimate is printed in the Bible?" asked Darrow.

"Everybody knows," said Bryan—"at least I think most of the people know—that was the estimate given."

"But what do you think the Bible itself says?" pursued Darrow. When Bryan hesitated, he asked: "Don't you know how it was arrived at?"

"I never made a calculation," said Bryan.

"A calculation from what?" asked Darrow.

"I could not say," admitted Bryan.

"From the generations of man?" offered Darrow.

"I would not want to say that."

"What do you think?" asked Darrow.

"I do not think about things I don't think about."

"Do you think about things you do think about?" cracked Darrow.

"Well, sometimes," said Bryan. The laughter of the crowd was so loud and long that the bailiff had to call for order.

Darrow often tried to discover the depth—or shallowness—of Bryan's learning. His quizzing often revealed a contrast between Darrow, who had read widely, and Bryan, who apparently had not—a contrast that eventually began to annoy Bryan. At one point Darrow asked Bryan about ancient civilizations. "Now, I ask you . . ." began Darrow, obviously trying to rankle Bryan, "if it was interesting enough or important enough for you to try to find out about how old these ancient civilizations were?"

"No," said Bryan. "I have not made a study of it."

"Don't you know," pressed Darrow, "that the ancient civilizations of China are six or seven thousand years old at the very least?"

"No," said Bryan. Then he added, faithful to Bishop Ussher: "But they would not run back beyond creation—according to the Bible, six thousand years."

"You don't know how old they are—is that right?" said Darrow.

"I don't know how old they are," said Bryan, annoyed. Then he added as the crowd laughed: "But probably you do!"

Darrow's questions goaded Bryan into trying to display his knowledge when he could. "What about the religion of Confucius or Buddha?" asked Darrow, trying to discover whether Bryan felt that any other religion competed with Christianity.

"Well, I can tell you something about that," said Bryan, "if you would like to know."

"Did you ever investigate them?"

"Somewhat," said Bryan.

"Do you regard them as competitive?"

"No, I think they are very inferior," said Bryan. "Would you like for me to tell you what I know about it?"

"No," said Darrow.

"Well, I shall insist on giving it to you," said Bryan.

"You won't talk about free silver, will you?"

"Not at all," said Bryan without cracking a smile. He found no humor in Darrow's gibe about his favorite topic for a speech during his first presidential campaign back in 1896.

Bryan eventually got his way and managed to slip in several speeches on Confucius and Buddha. "I object," Darrow finally protested to the judge, "to Mr. Bryan making a speech every time I ask him a question."

But soon Darrow got back to questions on the Bible. During much of the questioning Darrow sat on the edge of a table, his shoulders slouched, a Bible in his hands. Bryan sat in the witness chair holding his customary palm-leaf fan. "You have heard of the Tower of Babel, haven't you?" asked Darrow.

"Yes, sir."

"That tower was built under the ambition that they could build a tower to heaven, wasn't it?" continued Darrow. "And God saw what they were at, and to prevent their getting into heaven he confused their tongues?"

"Something like that," said Bryan, who then added to Darrow's explanation.

After some calculation based on Bishop Ussher's dates, they decided the tower-building had happened about 4155 years ago.

"Up to 4155 years ago," asked Darrow, "every human being on earth spoke the same language?"

"Yes, sir," said Bryan. "I think that is the inference that could be drawn from that."

"All the different languages of the earth dating from the Tower of Babel?" repeated Darrow. "Is that right?" Then he asked in an earnest tone: "Do you know how many languages are spoken on the face of the earth?"

"No," said Bryan. But he admitted there were hundreds. "I know the Bible has been translated into five hundred," he said proudly, " and no other book has been translated into anything like that many."

Soon Darrow was asking about the age of the earth: "Mr. Bryan, could you tell me how old the earth is?"

"No, sir. I couldn't." Bryan's palm-leaf fan moved more quickly.

"Could you come anywhere near it?"

"I wouldn't attempt to," said Bryan, showing an unexpected reluctance to answer the question. "I could possibly come as near as the scientists do," he added heatedly, "but I would rather be more accurate before I give a guess!"

Darrow's questioning led away from the age of the earth. But some of the audience were obviously confused.

Bryan accepted Bishop Ussher's idea that man was created in 4004 B.C. If the earth was assembled in six days, as the Bible says, with man appearing on the last of those days, didn't that answer the question of the earth's age? Darrow later returned to the question of the earth's age.

"Do you think the earth was made in six days?" asked Darrow.

"Not in six days of twenty-four hours," replied Bryan.

"Doesn't it say so?" asked Darrow in disbelief.

"No, sir."

The impact of Bryan's words was blunted by Stewart. "I want to interpose another objection. What is the purpose of this examination?" he challenged.

"The purpose is to cast ridicule on everybody who believes in the Bible," snarled Bryan, "and I am perfectly willing that the world shall know that these gentlemen have no other purpose than ridiculing every Christian who believes in the Bible!"

Darrow exploded: "We have the purpose of preventing bigots and ignoramuses from controlling the education of the United States and you know it! And that is all."

It was a while before the examination got back on the track, as Hays and Malone and Judge Raulston also entered the argument. But eventually Darrow was able to explore Bryan's beliefs again.

"Mr. Bryan, do you believe that the first woman was Eve?"

"Yes."

"Do you believe she was literally made out of Adam's rib?" went on Darrow.

"I do."

"Did you ever discover where Cain got his wife?"

"No, sir," said Bryan. "I leave the agnostics to hunt for her."

As the afternoon wore on, a breeze had sprung up that rustled the trees. It carried a strong hint of rain.

Presently Darrow got back to the six "days" of creation. "You think those were not literal days?" asked Darrow.

"I do not think they were 24-hour days," said Bryan. But he was careful not to rule out the possibility that the Bible did speak of literal days. "That is my opinion. I do not know that my opinion is better on that subject than those who think it does." Bryan seemed to be sensing that some of his followers in the audience were shocked by his belief.

"You do not think that?" continued Darrow.

"No," said Bryan. "But I think it would be just as easy for the kind of God we believe in to make the earth in six days as in six years or in six million years—or in six hundred million years. I do not think it important whether we believe one or the other."

If Darrow was beginning to have his doubts about the strength of Bryan's fundamentalism, he soon forgot them. "Do you believe that after Eve ate the apple, or gave it to Adam—whichever way it was—" said Darrow, "that God cursed Eve, and that time decreed that all womankind thenceforth and forever should suffer the pains of child-birth in the reproduction of the earth?"

"I believe what it says."

Questioning Bryan further about the story of Eve's temptation by the serpent, Darrow quoted the Bible he had in his hand: "And the Lord God said unto the serpent, Because thou hast done this, thou are cursed above all cattle, and above every beast of the field. Upon thy belly shalt thou go and dust shalt thou eat all the days of thy life." Then Darrow asked: "Do you think that is why the serpent is compelled to crawl upon its belly?"

"I believe that," said Bryan.

"Have you any idea how the snake went before that time?" asked Darrow.

"No, sir."

"Do you know whether he walked on his tail or not?"

"No, sir," said Bryan. "I have no way to know." The crowd chuckled.

Darrow began on another topic, but Bryan by now had had enough. "Your honor, I think I can shorten this testimony. The only purpose Mr. Darrow has is to slur at the Bible," said Bryan. "But I will answer his question. I will answer it all at once, and I have no objection in the world." Bryan and Darrow were now both on their feet glaring at each other. "I want the world to know that this man who does not believe in a God is trying to use a court in Tennessee . . ."

"I object to that!" spat Darrow.

". . . to slur at it," continued Bryan. "And while it will require time, I am willing to take it."

"I object to your statement," said Darrow. "I am examining you on your fool ideas that no intelligent Christian on earth believes!"

As Bryan and Darrow stood glaring at each other Judge Raulston brought down his gavel. "Court is adjourned until nine o'clock tomorrow morning." The Duel in the Shade, as Scopes later called it, was over.

CHAPTER THIRTEEN
VERDICT

After court had adjourned, Hutchinson, the INS reporter who had "leaked" the judge's decision on the motion to quash, grabbed Scopes by the arm and said: "Let's get to the press hall."

The newsmen had been given a room over the town's hardware store where they could type up their stories. Only half a dozen were there that afternoon. The rest who were still covering the trial had retreated to some cooler place such as the nearby resort town of Morgan Springs, where Scopes had been "romanced" the first Saturday night. Expecting the trial would end routinely, the missing newsmen had made arrangements with Hutchinson and the other reporters who attended the session to file stories for them.

Scopes found the operation fascinating but frustrating. Each of the reporters in the press hall typed his own story with five carbon copies. Then the reporters reworked the copies so that no two stories would read quite the same. Scopes tried to contribute to the press-hall activity, but did little more than make a decision about his future: "It was then that I learned I wasn't cut out to be a journalist. Writing under pressure of the day's deadline was not for me."

When a big enough batch of stories had been concocted to cover everybody, the reporters wired in their own stories. Then, being careful not to hurry too much, they wired in stories for their missing friends.

Darrow's examination of Bryan on the lawn of the Rhea County courthouse was destined to live on as the big event of the Scopes trial. "Those who had left early, such as Mencken, and those who had played hooky for the afternoon," Scopes later wrote, "had missed what some have called the most dramatic courtroom scene of the century."

But Scopes himself didn't agree. "I would save that exclusive description for Malone's response to Bryan on the preceding Thursday," he said, "which surpassed everything else I have seen or heard."

Tuesday, the eighth day of the trial, proved to be its last. If the "duelists" Bryan and Darrow had had their way, it wouldn't have been. Darrow hadn't run out of questions to ask, and Bryan was still anxious to examine Darrow— not to mention Malone and Hays. But Attorney General Stewart and Judge Raulston had other things in mind for the trial.

"I feel that the testimony of Mr. Bryan can shed no light upon any issues that will be pending before the higher courts," said Judge Raulston, soon after court was opened. A few minutes later he announced: "I am pleased to expunge this testimony, given by Mr. Bryan on yesterday, from the records of this court, and it will not be further considered."

Tuesday's session was back inside the courthouse. Rain on Monday evening had cooled Dayton enough to make the cracks in the ceiling below seem unimportant. The early part of the session was spent with details—mostly Hays "getting the record straight" so there would be no hitch in the appeal. Bryan and Darrow did manage to have a short argument, though.

Bryan seemed concerned about how his examination the day before would be handled in the court record. "Now, I had not reached the point where I could make a statement to answer the charges made by the counsel for the defense," he said, "as to my ignorance and my bigotry."

"I object, your honor," said Darrow, not really sure what he was objecting to. "Now what's all this about?"

"Why do you want to make this, Colonel Bryan?" asked the judge, who was confused himself.

"I just want to finish my sentence," said Bryan.

"Why can't he go outside on the lawn?" said Darrow, who obviously smelled another Bryan speech.

Bryan, it developed, was simply pleading for a hearing in the press. His examination by Darrow could be "expunged" from the court record, but it was already well recorded in the nation's press. He wanted his turn to examine Darrow and the rest—in the press, if not in court. "I think it is only fair," challenged Bryan, "that the country should know the religious attitude of the people who come down here to deprive the people of Tennessee of the right to run their own schools."

After Bryan had spoken his piece, matters moved quickly. The prosecution and the defense and the judge had a private talk and decided there was no point in prolonging the proceedings. With their game of examining each other declared out of order by the judge, the lawyers on both sides decided there really wasn't anything else to say that had any bearing on the case.

After a short recess while the judge dictated his instructions for the jury, the twelve jurors were called in for another of their rare appearances in the trial. Judge Raulston read his instructions, which contained many words but only one significant instruction: "The court charges you that in order to prove its case the State does not have to specifically prove that the defendant taught a theory that denied the story of the divine creation of man as taught in the Bible, other than to prove that he taught that man descended from a lower order of animals."

Darrow then rose to address the jury. Usually his job would be to argue his client's innocence. But not today. "We cannot argue to you gentlemen under the instructions given by the court," said Darrow. "We cannot even explain to you that we think you should return a verdict of not guilty. We do not see how you could. We do not ask it. We think we will save our point and take it to the higher court and settle whether the law is good, and also whether he should have permitted the evidence. I guess that is plain enough."

Legal arguments about Scopes's fine followed. Judge Raulston had told the jury that they didn't have to decide on the fine unless they felt it should be more than the minimum $100. Stewart wasn't sure that was right, but didn't make a big issue of it. At the time, it seemed an unimportant technicality.

Attorney General Stewart then had a few words to say to the jury—not more than three sentences. Just in case they hadn't understood the plain talk of Mr. Darrow, he made it even plainer: "What Mr. Darrow wanted to say to you was that he wanted you to find his client guilty, but did not want to be in the position of pleading guilty, because it would destroy his rights in the appellate court."

The jury was then sent out for "deliberation." Nine minutes later, their deliberation over, the jury returned with their verdict. "We have found for the State," announced the foreman, "found the defendant guilty." The fine, he explained, they left to the judge.

"Mr. Scopes, will you come around here, please, sir." His moment had come. John Thomas Scopes, spectator defendant, was at last to play a part in this great courtroom drama.

Following the tradition of the courts, Judge Raulston explained to Scopes what he already well knew: what the jury had done and what offense he had committed. "The court now fixes your fine at $100," concluded Raulston, "and imposes that fine upon you . . ."

But before Raulston could finish imposing the penalty, Neal, the Tennessee defense counsel, interrupted: "May it please your honor, he wants to be heard a moment." Among the traditions of sentencing, Raulston had overlooked one.

"Oh," said Raulston. "Have you anything to say, Mr. Scopes, as to why the court should not impose punishment upon you?"

"Your honor, I feel that I have been convicted of violating an unjust statute," said Scopes. It was a spur-of-the-moment thing, he later said, but he seemed to find the right words. "I will continue in the future, as I have in the past, to oppose this law in any way I can. Any other action would be in violation of my ideal of academic freedom—that is, to teach the truth as guaranteed in our constitution —of personal and religious freedom. I think the fine is unjust."

The judge then imposed the penalty—the $100 fine already announced, and costs, which came to about three times the fine—and that was the end of it. Of course there were a few technicalities.

And of course there were a few "farewell addresses." Several representatives of the newsmen had friendly words to say about Dayton. Then the younger McKenzie had friendly words for the newsmen: "We have been greatly elevated, edified, and educated by your presence. And should the time ever come when you are back near the garden spot of the world, we hope that you will stop off and stay a while with us here in order that we may chat about the days of the past when the Scopes trial was tried in Dayton."

Bryan said a few words, too, though his mood was too serious to permit pleasantries: "Here has been fought out a little case of little consequence as a case. But the world is interested because it raises an issue. And that issue will some day be settled right. Whether it is settled on our side or the other side, it is going to be settled right."

Darrow followed, speaking in his usual chatty, wise-cracking fashion. He thanked the Tennessee lawyers for their courtesy and he thanked the judge for not sending him to jail for contempt. And then he made a short speech: "I think this case will be remembered because it is the first case of this sort since we stopped trying people in America for witchcraft—because here we have done our best to turn back the tide that has sought to force itself upon this modern world, of testing every fact in science by a religious dictum."

The judge wound up the festivities with a speech of his own. But the last word was really had by Arthur Garfield Hays. "May I, as one of the counsel for the defense," said Hays, "ask your honor to allow me to send you the *The Origin of Species* and the *The Descent of Man,* by Charles Darwin?"

"Yes, yes," said Judge Raulston, as the courtroom rocked with laughter and applause.

And then it was over. "We will adjourn," said Judge Raulston, "and Brother Jones will pronounce the benediction."

"May the grace of our Lord Jesus Christ, the love of God, and the communion and fellowship of the Holy Ghost abide with you all. Amen."

CHAPTER FOURTEEN
THE WAYS OF
GOD AND MAN

For William Jennings Bryan the Dayton trial didn't really end on that Tuesday when the final benediction was intoned. He had planned two events that hadn't happened during the trial. He decided they should happen anyway.

One was his examination of Darrow. He had hoped to get Darrow to make a public confession of his sinful ideas about God and the Bible. But the quick ending of the trial had kept him from showing how wicked a man his opponent was.

The day after the trial Bryan asked his questions anyway. And Darrow answered them. "Do you believe in the existence of God as described in the Bible?" Bryan began, and ran through nine questions. Only the last seemed to be any challenge to the theory of evolution: "If you believe in evolution, at what point in man's descent from the brute is he endowed with hope and promise of a life beyond the grave?"

The agnostic Darrow was happy to reveal his "wickedness." The word "agnostic" comes from two Greek words meaning "without knowledge." And Darrow's sin, if it was one, was his quickness to confess his lack of knowledge. "I do not know of any description of God in the Bible," he began his first answer, and his other answers struck the same note. His last answer showed how open a mind he had in matters of religion. "I have no knowledge on the question of when man first believed in life beyond the grave," he said. "I am not at all sure whether some other animals have not the same hope of future life." Then he added: "Its origin may have arisen in vivid dreams concerning the return of the dead or, from all I know, from actual evidences of the return of the dead."

For Bryan, the examination fizzled. If it did anything, it showed Darrow to be a more reasonable man than the fundamentalists had pictured him. The questions and answers of Bryan's little examination were duly reported by the newspapers, and then forgotten.

The other unfinished business for Bryan was his final argument to the jury. This, many had decided, would be another Cross of Gold speech. The Bryan that stirred the 1896 Democratic convention to nominate him for president might even now, in his speech to the jury, stir the common people throughout the country to take up the fight against evolution.

As it happened, Bryan himself had spoiled his chance to deliver the speech. By arguing against expert testimony, he robbed the defense of its last chance to save John Scopes from conviction. When the defense then called it quits, Bryan was silenced. His great speech to the jury, which took two months to prepare, went undelivered.

Bryan, though, couldn't let it go at that. He made arrangements to have the speech printed in a Chattanooga newspaper. Then on Saturday he tried out the speech before two different groups—not the whole speech, but good-sized parts of it.

Bryan was still full of talk. Some who had seen him since the trial had decided he was "a crushed and broken man." But his activities didn't look like those of a crushed and broken man. Now that antievolution had won the day in Tennessee—or so he argued—Bryan was getting set to sell it to the nation. The next step was to get an amendment to the United States constitution making the teaching of evolution unconstitutional.

But it was a step he would never take. On Sunday morning Bryan led the congregation in prayer at a Methodist church in Dayton. After the service he returned to the home where he had been staying while in Dayton to have Sunday dinner. Afterwards he went upstairs to nap, for the meal had been large. Bryan never rose from his nap. He suffered a stroke as he slept and died without waking.

To many fundamentalists, Bryan had died defending the Bible—the revealed word of God. He was a martyr pure and simple. The great strain of resisting the vicious attack of the infidel Darrow had been too much for his aging body.

Scopes, though, had a different answer. It was the great strain of overeating that he blamed. Bryan was almost as well known for his ability to eat as for his ability to speak. During his campaign of 1900, a reporter noted what Bryan had for breakfast one morning in Virginia: "An enormous melon, two quails, a formidable slice of ham with six eggs, batter cakes immersed in butter, accompanied here and there with potatoes and small delicacies for side dishes, all of which he washed down with innumerable cups of coffee with milk."

In his later years Bryan had developed diabetes and was under doctor's orders not to eat sugar or starch. And Scopes had noticed that at the banquet before the trial, Bryan had carefully avoided bread. His gesture amused Scopes, though, for he ate heartily of other starch-laden foods. In fact, when Bryan noticed that Scopes wasn't touching his potatoes or corn, Bryan asked: "John, are you going to eat your side dishes?" Since John wasn't, Bryan took on another load of forbidden starch. "No reasonable man would call his a martyr's death," decided Scopes. "His eating habits must have, in some way, hastened his death."

For John Scopes the first week after the trial was a time for housecleaning. Scopes had been getting mail by the washtub—literally. As the front porch of the house where he stayed piled higher with letters, Scopes decided that a bonfire was the only answer. Two friends helped him haul armloads of letters out into the yard where they could be burned.

As the fire blazed, now and again one of the three would rake out an unburned letter, read it, and toss it back into the flames. Marriage proposals, offers to lecture on evolution on the vaudeville stage, movie contracts—all went up in smoke. "Many newspaper stories reported I had been offered all kinds of fortunes and movie contracts and God knows what else," Scopes later reported. "Probably they were accurate."

Scopes never knew how many movie contracts or job offers or marriage proposals went up in smoke.

Scopes was running away from the trial as fast as he could. He had been just a bit player in the drama of Bryan versus Darrow, and he wanted to keep it that way. "I had only one life in this world and I wanted to enjoy it," he said later. "I knew I could not live happily in a spotlight."

One offer that came as a result of the trial he accepted. Fearing that the trial had cost him his old job, the expert witnesses had gotten together a scholarship fund large enough to give him a couple more years of college. He could study whatever he wanted to.

Scopes's choice, he thought, was law. He was already well started toward a law degree and shouldn't have much trouble finishing in the two years. So on the weekend after the close of the trial he went to the University of Kentucky to talk with the dean of the law school about returning there to get his law degree. The dean thought it was a fine idea. He could be another Darrow!

The dean was trying to encourage Scopes to continue law. But quite innocently he had succeeded in turning him away from it. As a lawyer Scopes's name would always bring to mind Darrow's. Could he stand being forever compared with the great Darrow? To walk "in the shadow of another man's fame," he decided, was not what he wanted. He wanted to be himself.

In the end, being himself meant giving up Kentucky as well as law. After discarding law, he quickly chose geology, which was another subject that had intrigued him as an undergraduate. But Kentucky didn't offer an advanced degree in geology.

And so in the fall of 1925 John Scopes did not return from a lazy summer in Paducah to coach the students of Rhea County Central High School in the art of football. Instead he entered the University of Chicago as a graduate student in geology. Dayton's "long hot summer" had made its first mark on his life.

During the two years that Scopes spent at the University of Chicago, the legal tail end of the Scopes trial ran its leisurely course. After some delay the appeal was argued before the Tennessee supreme court in Nashville in June 1926, almost a year after the Dayton trial. It was no Monkey Trial this time—no clash of champions before cheering multitudes. But one of the champions of Dayton was there. Clarence Darrow again was on hand.

Darrow's appearance in Nashville came about in much the same way as his appearance in Dayton. Scopes argued for him. The ACLU thought a more stately, stolid man would make a better showing before the high court. But Scopes couldn't see it that way. Darrow surely was more familiar with the case than any newcomer.

Darrow's arguments before the supreme court had a familiar ring, of course. It was mostly a matter of rehashing the old arguments for a new audience. And of course he did not spare the high court a quip or two. But his defense of the right to learn was as vigorous and as serious as ever.

"It may be that a little learning is a dangerous thing, and a great deal of learning is fatal," he admitted at one point. "But in spite of that, as long as man has an inquiring mind, he will seek to know and to find out." Then Darrow added, with obvious conviction: "And every child ought to be more intelligent than his parents."

The decision was long delayed. Fall politics seemed to be in the way of saying yes or no about such a touchy matter. The decision was finally announced on January 14, 1927—if you could call it a decision.

The supreme court of Tennessee had five justices. Two of the five agreed with the verdict reached in Dayton. The Butler Act, these justices felt, was constitutional, and John Scopes had broken it. The third justice, though, didn't see it quite that way. In his opinion, the Butler Act didn't outlaw teaching evolution entirely. It only outlawed teaching that God was nowhere involved in man's creation. Evolution might be taught in the public schools as long as it wasn't a wholly godless evolution. Since it had not been shown that Scopes had denied God's hand in the evolutionary goings-on, he was innocent of the charges.

The fourth justice also found Scopes innocent, though for a simpler reason. In his opinion the law was too vague. It should be ruled unconstitutional, he felt, and Scopes cleared.

That seemed to leave Scopes's fate in the hands of the fifth justice. But there was a hitch. The fifth justice was new to the court and didn't feel he could be involved. And so the verdict seemed to be hung—two votes for Scopes, two against. A new appeal seemed called for.

But through a clever legal move, that new appeal never happened. The justices decided that Judge Raulston had acted improperly in setting the fine of $100. According to the Tennessee constitution, any fine of more than $50 had to be set by the jury. And so they overruled Scopes's conviction.

Usually that would have meant another trial—another long hot Dayton summer! But the justices didn't want that, they decided. "We see nothing to be gained," wrote the chief justice, "by prolonging the life of this bizarre case." He then suggested that the attorney general drop the charges and forget the whole affair.

And so it ended. The defense had hoped to have the Butler Act declared unconstitutional. They fully expected to take the case to the United States supreme court if Tennessee upheld the law. But now there was no case any more—nothing to appeal.

And so after all the trouble, John Scopes unhappily found himself innocent of crime. His efforts to be officially branded a violator of the Butler Act had in the end failed. But having failed to be convicted of his crime, Scopes was soon to discover that he was still a criminal in the minds of some people.

CHAPTER FIFTEEN
FLIGHT FROM FAME

To the people of Dayton the name of Scopes had meant a soft-spoken, pleasant schoolteacher that everybody liked. And even though he smoked and danced, he wasn't really a sinner to most people who knew him. He even went to Church on Sunday. But away from Dayton, the name of Scopes had taken on a different meaning. To some people, at least, it had become a symbol of godlessness.

As Scopes studied at Chicago, he became increasingly aware of the burden of his name. Since he had fought a battle for education, his name was especially well-known in educational circles. And that should have helped him, you would think. But his fame in those circles, he decided, was not always a benefit. "The monkey on my back was the Dayton trial," he wrote, "and I would not be allowed to forget it, especially if I stayed in education." He had thought that he might become a teacher of geology but was changing his mind.

What convinced him most that he should shun teaching as a profession was something that happened during the spring of his second year at Chicago. The professor who directed his study there had recommended him for a scholarship. It was something he wanted badly, and he was delighted to have the recommendation. The scholarship would have given him enough money to complete his studies toward a Ph.D. in geology.

But the scholarship was not to be his. The Dayton trial came back to plague him. "Your name has been removed from consideration for the fellowship," the head of the scholarship fund wrote. "As far as I am concerned," he added, "you can take your atheistic marbles and play elsewhere."

Scopes was dismayed. The writer of those words was the president of a well-known university. How many other university people might feel as he did? Perhaps Scopes had run into an unusual educator. But he didn't think so. "I knew if that university, one of the most respected in the United States, was like that," he said, "then I would be better off going into commercial work and ignoring the academic world entirely." Being the notorious John Scopes, he decided, would be a great handicap to a teacher. It had surely proved a great handicap as a student, for now he was forced to drop out of school.

And so as John Scopes contemplated the summer of 1927, he couldn't help but feel hounded by his past. The bonfire he had lit two summers before had not marked the end of his notoriety, as he had hoped it would. Was there any escape?

Fleeing to the steaming jungles of South America would seem to be carrying things too far. And maybe Scopes didn't think of it quite that way. But in the summer of 1927 he took a job in Venezuela as a geologist for a large oil company, a job that would send him into those jungles. He later admitted that what he had most wanted was to be "just another man instead of the Monkey Trial defendant." In the Venezuelan jungles maybe he could. He signed for three years.

In the 17th century it was often gold that attracted people to Maracaibo and made it a favorite target of pi-

rates. In the 20th century it was "black gold" that drew men to the still thriving city. Maracaibo lies in the northwest corner of Venezuela at the point where the Lake of Maracaibo joins the sea. The earliest explorers found oil seeping from the ground along the shores of the lake. Now that supply was being drawn off, and modern explorers were looking for more, Scopes became one of them.

The oil company had offices in Maracaibo and Scopes could have worked there. But he chose instead to work in the field making geological surveys. What his job amounted to was making maps that would be helpful to the oil company in deciding where to drill for oil. Knowing the kinds of soil and the kinds of rocks that were found in various places, a geologist could predict where oil was most likely to be found. So for Scopes, Venezuela meant months of wandering about the wilds.

Lonesome and bored, Scopes had been in Venezuela over a year when he became the unwilling host for one of the numerous tropical germs. His woes began when a small wound on the little finger of his left hand became infected, swelling his whole arm and even part of his chest. Then the germs of dysentery and malaria gained a hold in his weakened body. After several weeks in a Maracaibo hospital, he was sent back to the United States to recover.

Scopes hardly reached America before he decided to leave again. But this time he wasn't fleeing his reputation. His lingering diseases didn't bother him much once he was out of the tropics. "Convalescing back in the States," he admitted, "I was more active than I had been in South

America." And so he quickly decided to take his Cockney father back to England for a visit.

Scopes had left Venezuela in December fully convinced that he would never go back to his job there. His three-year stretch was only half spent, but he decided he had no taste for life in the jungle. But the trip with his father changed all that, for it used up most of the money he had saved from his Venezuela experience. Soon after his return from England in June, his company wired that they had a reservation for him on a Venezuela-bound ship. He took it.

At first, Scopes managed to keep out of the jungle that he had grown to dislike. He was assigned to the company office in Maracaibo. The job might not have been more interesting, but the surroundings certainly were. At a country-club dance one night he met "a pretty brown-eyed brunette from South Carolina" named Mildred Walker.

Southerner Mildred Walker at once recognized John Scopes as the notorious defendant in the Monkey Trial. But she soon decided that wasn't really a serious flaw. "My aunt thought that Scopes was something with horns on," she later admitted. "I never dreamed then that I would meet him and marry him!" They were married in February of 1930 in Maracaibo.

For Scopes, marriage was another brush with religion —not fundamentalism, this time, but Catholicism. To please his Catholic wife-to-be, he joined her religion so that they could be married in her church. But his new "faith" proved not to be deep. "The priest in Maracaibo surely realized I couldn't accept everything he told me I should believe," he later commented. "A good agnostic couldn't give up his faith that easily."

The Scopeses' honeymoon was short. Soon after their marriage Scopes sent Mildred back to the United States while he went off into the jungles again. His luck had run out. The job this time was to survey the land near the border of Colombia—even over the border. His company wasn't permitted to enter Colombia, but he had orders to do so anyway. If he got caught, though, he was on his own. The company couldn't afford to admit that he had orders from them to break the law.

It was about a month before the expedition reached the border. Then for two weeks Scopes hesitated, struggling with his conscience. In the end he decided not to cross. "I had been married only a short time," he explained, "and I had been sent to this godforsaken backwoods of the world. What if I were arrested and slapped into some obscure dank cell? Would anyone ever hear of me again?" The married Scopes was not so quick to break the law of Colombia as the bachelor Scopes had been to break the law of Tennessee.

"When I got back to Maracaibo," Scopes reported, "the chief geologist told me the company was cutting down on expenses and that, unfortunately, I was one expense they didn't need." What they didn't need, Scopes decided, was a man who would obey somebody else's law instead of the company's instructions. So as the summer of 1930 came on, John Scopes was once again returning home.

For Scopes the fall of 1930 looked much like the fall of 1925. He was five years older, it's true, and married. But he was back at the University of Chicago working toward a Ph.D. in geology. And he again had enough money, he thought, to support a couple years of schooling.

Scopes's decision to go back to school seemed strange after his earlier flight from the academic world. But in 1930 America was in the midst of a severe business depression and jobs of any sort were hard to get. Times might improve in two years. And if they didn't, a Ph.D. after his name might open more doors.

Returning to Chicago meant seeing Clarence Darrow again. Scopes had been a frequent visitor at the Darrow house during his earlier bachelor days at the University. Darrow was in the habit of inviting Chicago professors and sometimes their graduate students to dinner and conversation. Usually Scopes would join them. The Darrows, in fact, had encouraged him to drop around whenever he felt like it. Now back in Chicago, Scopes was able to renew his friendship with the Darrows as a married man.

Scopes's view of Darrow was quite simple: "Darrow was a genius." And his view was shared by many who knew him well. One of the science professors at Chicago commented: "If Darrow had applied himself to any scientific field, he would have been outstanding in it, regardless of which one he had chosen." Scopes never regretted his choice of Darrow to defend him in Dayton. And surely among the larger rewards of his days in Chicago were his frequent contacts with the brilliant lawyer.

But Chicago kept some of its prizes beyond Scopes's grasp. The Ph.D. again escaped him. Two years after his second return the money had run out again with the degree still not quite in hand. And with a wife soon to give birth to his first child, Scopes decided there were more important matters to worry about than an elusive Ph.D.

When John Thomas Scopes, Jr., was born in the fall of 1932, John Thomas Scopes, Sr., was looking for a job. The two years since his return had not brought better times. Jobs were still hard to find. It was the following summer before Scopes found one. In the summer of 1933 he went to work for another oil company—in Texas this time.

Scopes never returned to get his Ph.D. Soon after the move to Texas, the birth of William Scopes made the Scopeses a family of four. With a good job and a happy family, the Ph.D. became a meaningless goal. Scopes settled down to "normal, ordinary work characteristic of any large oil and gas company." The job took Scopes to Shreveport, Louisiana, in 1940. There he spent the last thirty years of his life as John Scopes, ordinary citizen.

But John Scopes was not the name of an ordinary citizen to the rest of the world. Dayton's "long hot summer" of 1925 had fixed that.

CHAPTER SIXTEEN
RETURN OF A HERO

July has usually been the worst time," said Scopes, "as people remember it was the month of the Dayton trial." He was talking about the mail he got from strangers during his years in Shreveport. Many letters were simply requests for autographs. Many others, though, were more earnest. They were often from preachers or other religious people bent on reforming Scopes. The story of how they had "got religion," some of these thought, might give him some good ideas. Or perhaps a quotation from the Bible might work some special magic with the infidel Scopes.

Mail was also brisk in April or May as the school year was ending and term papers were being written. But Scopes refused to help the students with their assignments. There were just too many of them.

If the memory of the Scopes trial was fading over the years, it wasn't obvious. But if it needed refreshment, it got it as the thirtieth anniversary of the trial approached. On April 22, 1955, a play called *Inherit the Wind* opened on Broadway. The play revolved around an earnest young teacher named Bertram Cates, who had been locked up in the Hillsboro jail for teaching the theory of evolution in the local school.

"*Inherit the Wind* is not history," explained the writers of the play. But they still wanted everyone to know what event of history had inspired it. "The events which took place in Dayton, Tennessee, during the scorching July of 1925 are clearly the genesis of the play," they admitted. "It has, however," they added, "an exodus entirely its own."

Bert Cates, the John Scopes of the play, had a more upsetting time than his real-life model. Not only was he held in jail for his offense, but he had a good prospect of staying there. And worst of all, he was in love with the daughter of the town's fundamentalist preacher!

The prosecution in the case against Cates was led by Attorney General Tom Davenport, who was assisted by the great Matthew Harrison Brady, three-time loser in the presidential election. Defending poor Bert was a famous criminal lawyer, well known for his agnosticism, Henry Drummond. And of course the trial scene wouldn't have been complete without an acid-tongued journalist around to make sarcastic comments about the local citizens. An important character in the play was a journalist from Baltimore named E. K. Hornbeck.

Cates came out of it all with only a fine of $100—true to life. But then he ran off with his girl. Matthew Harrison Brady, less durable than his real-life model, was reduced to a gibbering idiot at trial's end and promptly collapsed and died right then.

Scopes never saw this stage version of his trial. "I'd been too busy," he explained, "and not interested enough to fly to New York and see it." But when a movie was made from the play five years later, he had a change of heart. The producer of the movie—with the help of Mildred Scopes—talked him into promoting the film. And so in July of 1960 on the 35th anniversary of the trial, Scopes returned to the scene of his youthful "crime," for the movie premiere was held in Dayton.

Thirty-five years had left few of the trial's participants alive. Some of the students that Scopes had taught were still around. A few of the jurors survived. Sue Hicks, one of the prosecution lawyers, was there—now a judge. But the main cast was absent. Bryan, of course, had died. So had Clarence Darrow, who would have been 103 by then. And so had the other defense lawyers, Malone, Hays, and Neal. Death had also taken Judge Raulston.

Doc Robinson was gone, but his drugstore wasn't. In 35 years its prices had changed a good deal—with one temporary exception. "Scopes Soda 15¢" read a new sign. "Priced Now as Then in Honor of Scopes' Return to Dayton."

The mayor of Dayton proclaimed a Scopes Trial Day, and gave Scopes a key to the city. But Scopes wondered how many of the local citizens really welcomed him. On the morning of Scopes Trial Day a Tennessee preacher on the radio warned: "The devil is here in Dayton and is having a heyday."

Scopes was clearly a "reluctant ballyhooist," as one reporter described him. And when the premiere was over he settled quietly back into his Shreveport routine.

A picture of John Scopes of Shreveport can be gotten from an interview in the fall of 1962. "Gone are the smooth-faced boyish look, the horn-rimmed glasses . . ." wrote the interviewer. "Now his face is weatherbeaten from years outdoors, and the wrinkles confirm his sixty-two years. He is slightly stooped. His suit is casually worn, and he holds a cigarette—an item he is seldom seen without."

The interviewer tried to turn the conversation to the Scopes trial: "I discover he has not wasted time thinking about the trial. I speak of persons I have read about in connection with the trial; he isn't sure he remembers them. I recall things he said at the time of the trial; yes, he remembers that . . . but he'd forgotten that was the way he had said it. It is not a matter of bad memory; it is a matter of what John Scopes has considered important . . ."

But as Scopes's life moved toward its final years, the "reluctant ballyhooist" began to lose some of his reluctance. In 1964 he retired from his oil-company job, and with retirement he seemed to find his voice.

"If I had been asked the last day of the trial what had been accomplished, I would have been a most embarrassed lad," he began an article that was printed in a 1965 book about the trial. But forty years later Scopes thought he could answer the question. "I feel that restrictive legislation on academic freedom is forever a thing of the past."

But Scopes, now turning his thoughts anew to such questions, may have spoken too quickly. For a year later he wrote: "Each generation, each person must defend these freedoms or risk losing them forever." Scopes wrote those words in the preface to a book about his life—his "memoirs."

Like the biblical Samson who regained his strength when his shorn hair grew long again, Scopes seemed now at last to be regaining the crusading spirit that had carried him into the courtroom in Dayton in 1925. The crusader, who seemed to have been shorn of his spirit by the Dayton trial and its aftermath, was finding it again in retirement.

Scopes's new crusade carried him back to Tennessee once again. On April 1, 1970, he found himself inside a Tennessee classroom for the first time in 45 years. He had been invited to talk to a group of biology students at the George Peabody College for Teachers in Nashville, Tennessee.

Scopes was greeted in Tennessee "like a returning hero," wrote *Time* magazine. He was given "the long-delayed evidence that his battle for academic freedom had been successful," reported *Time:* "a copy of the 1967 state law repealing the old antievolution statute." After 42 years on the books, the Butler Act that had sent him to court had been repealed only three years before his visit.

What the "returning hero" had to say to his Nashville audience had a familiar ring. John Scopes in 1925 had risen in a Tennessee courtroom to announce: "I will continue in the future, as I have in the past, to oppose this law in any way I can. Any other action would be in violation of my ideal of academic freedom." John Scopes in 1970 rose in a Tennessee classroom to announce: "It is the teacher's business to decide what to teach. It is not the business of the federal courts nor of the state." It sounded like the same man. But there was an interesting difference. In 1925 Scopes was on the side of science. In 1970 he was on the side of religion.

Scopes hadn't changed. It was the law of the land that had changed. In 1925 the Butler Act made it against the law to talk about evolution in the classroom. But now in 1970, protested Scopes, decisions of the Supreme Court had made it against the law to pray in the classroom. "If I were teaching school and the only way I could communicate with the class was through prayer," said Scopes, "I would pray. And it would be none of the Supreme Court's business." The old Scopes had a new target.

But his new fight for academic freedom was to be cut short. That was his last public appearance. Later in 1970 John Scopes died. On October 21 in Shreveport he fell to cancer. His remains were returned to his first home of Paducah, Kentucky, for burial.

The story of John Scopes is the story of perhaps the world's most famous bystander. As one of the most dramatic battles for freedom of thought raged about him, Scopes remained little more than an interested spectator. It was a drama he could enjoy and applaud. But he never felt he could really participate. Toward the close of his seventy years he began to find his voice. But he spent most of his life trying to shake what he had called "the monkey on my back."

The blustering whirlwind has at its center an eye of quiet air. The Monkey Trial—the blustering "circus" that came to Dayton one hot summer—had at its center the quiet John Thomas Scopes.

INDEX

About the Author

D. C. Ipsen began his professional life as a research engineer in industry. Later, he moved into the field of education, first as engineering professor at the University of California, afterwards as curriculum developer in the same university's Elementary School Science Project. He is a graduate of the University of Michigan and holds a Ph.D. in mechanical engineering from the University of California at Berkeley.

Mr. Ipsen is the author of four successful books, WHAT DOES A BEE SEE?, THE ELUSIVE ZEBRA, THE RIDDLE OF THE STEGOSAURUS, and RATTLESNAKES AND SCIENTISTS.

About the Artist

Richard Cuffari has illustrated more than 40 books for children. A graduate of Pratt Institute, he has received awards from the Society of Illustrators and the American Institute of Graphic Arts.

Mr. Cuffari and his wife and their four children live in Brooklyn, New York.